Collected Later Poems

Christopher Middleton was bor
He studied at Merton College,
University of Zurich, at King's
Professor of Germanic Languag~~ ~~ ~~~ ~~~~~~~
Austin. He has published translations of Robert Walser,
Nietzsche, Hölderlin, Goethe, Gert Hofmann and many others.
Over the last two decades Carcanet has published six books of
his poems, one book of his experimental prose and two volumes
of essays, as well as his *Selected Writings* and *Faint Harps and Silver
Voices*, a collection of verse translations. He has received various
awards, including the Geoffrey Faber Memorial Prize, the
Schlegel-Tieck Translation Prize, and in 2012 an Award for
Literature from the American Academy of Arts and Letters.

Also by Christopher Middleton from Carcanet Press

Collected Poems
The Anti-Basilisk
The Word Pavilion
Jackdaw Jiving
Intimate Chronicles
The Balcony Tree
Selected Writings
Two Horse Wagon Going By
111 Poems
The Pursuit of the Kingfisher

As translator

Faint Harps and Silver Voices
Gert Hofmann, *The Spectacle at the Tower*
Gert Hofmann, *Our Conquest*
Robert Walser, *Selected Stories*

Christopher Middleton

Collected Later Poems

CARCANET

First published in Great Britain in 2014 by
Carcanet Press Limited
Alliance House
Cross Street
Manchester M2 7AQ

www.carcanet.co.uk

A CIP catalogue record for this book is available from the British Library

ISBN 978 1 84777 152 0

The publisher acknowledges financial assistance from Arts Council England

Supported by
ARTS COUNCIL
ENGLAND

Typeset by XL Publishing Services, Exmouth
Printed and bound in England by SRP Ltd, Exeter

Contents

The Tenor on Horseback

Poems 2006–2009

The Enjoyment of Shouting

A Company of Ghosts

1

2

3

Forty Days in the Calypso Saloon

1 From the Papers of Esteban Seferiades

Frescoes with Graffiti

Two Poems Mistakenly Omitted from *Collected Poems*

Three Tributes

Interim

The Tenor on Horseback

For Preface a Lacuna

Study the shoes Saint Francis left
At the edge of a forest when
On a whim he took to the trees –

New shoes? Shoes medieval, from the cow.
Elegant? Too strict for a man-at-arms?
Down at heel? To the Pope had been a long walk.

Seams burst, a toecap comes loose.
Well might we wonder at those particular shoes
And the thorn in the flesh, once the saint

Had got real. Study the hair no less: Fotis
Beside the bed lets loose a torrential
Chevelure, token of a carnal flux –

And in the morning Lucius was an ass. Hoofs are
Harder still to shed than footwear.
Hafis drank in Shiraz with a demon: Hair again,

Wings of flesh, precisely how should he extend
Favour to a girl, her braid, without analogy?
Cryptic, shining in the fibres, Allah danced...

Tell me flat that hair and shoe hold good;
Feet convenient, nothing to be damned about,
Hair no icon to induce a rapture with;

Yet to go bald by the rules of evidence,
To feel the thorn pierce only one of two feet,
How steep must be the slope a body slithers down?

On the forest edge, shoes intricately stitched.
Wait one moment, birds. Look, look into this.
Then tweeting, agile, out of the fresco flit.

The Part of Gravity

As if to gravity the one were not
   subject enough, the other
like a turtle cosying up

   for coitus but doomed to slip
slants across the exposed
   level surface of it,

two big stones, and both, submerged
   in shallow river water,
must have been made

   substance by fire and a tremendous
pressure, to the start of time
   closer far than yesterday –

Where was I now? calling to mind
   the killed in heaps, and 1848
in Alexander Herzen's ear

   the tocsin clanging from a steeple,
fractured first, then engulfed
   by frenzied act, the fine intention,

then to foresee the microbe of revenge
   drag revolution for the future
ranting to the ground…

   Inestimable muck, and little
grains of golden sand, together
   bed the stones, today a flood,

tomorrow all serene, even limpid
   the river, it may welcome
slender craft, where sit

stooping forward, straining back
    to suit their tension to the oars
they grip, the scullers.

The Poem Lost

There came a prompting to write a contrapuntal
And possibly syllabic poem –
It would mature from consideration of an oak tree
As portrayed by Delacroix and celebrated
In his *Journal*, combined (unfancifully)

With Joseph Conrad's descriptions of the sea
In his deep-etched essays, where old ships
Shift under sail with the winds to batter
Or bless them across the sea, at the mercy,
The undependable mercy of the sea.

Some way into the poem the oak
Would become a ship, and the old designers,
The ship-architects, would figure, while sounds
Such as the sea makes in a merciful mood
Would have coupled with the rustle of foliage.

There would also be acorns, battles, a typhoon
And doubtless a crow's nest between the lines;
But on discovering that I was only a cabin-boy,
Spontaneous, but not sufficiently intimate
With raw solids and liquid rage, I wrote this.

Body Count

While a lutenist is telling on the radio
How compositions for his instrument
Still answer needs (not only musical)
Felt by people now, more fully, even,
Than hip-hop or rockabilly of the moment,

I am left wondering at the open door
How old needs, huge with delusion,
Bubble up for ever from an aching hollow,
And why new needs? They do not roll back
A craving for Oh you know what...

Keen for a Pickering hornpipe, even sooner,
A mockingbird, a bluejay, and a wren
Had flitted up and perched,
Tilting their heads, on the balcony rail –
They breezed away, quick to be body still.

Into this tune, this fugue, this tangle, what
Was not condensed? If I listen harder,
Footsteps of women, children, crossing the Tigris
Make the bridge hum. At a detonation
Panicking back – this bloody crush, and in it

The number (not confirmable) of the maimed.

A Pair of Herons

No matter what it means,
I saw a pair of herons.
White, they flew upwind,

Upriver. White, against
A scree of sombre green
Tall trees, rock outcrops,

I saw them flying. If
The wind got brisk and blew
Their breastbone fluff apart

They reeled, sideslipping.
Then each would caracol,
To luff at any lull.

I saw them reeling, each
Easily righting itself
And flying, flying on.

So contraries collide,
For when I saw that pair
My worm writhed in their rose,

But vanishes like a nose
Now I, interpellated,
Imagine them still there.

A Sonnet of Nice Goats

Daredevil skateboard boys, they
  Scoot along a sidewalk.
And of a vacant floodlit tunnel
  They conceive, of whirling, heavens,
Across the roof. When a shot
  Rings out from the ghost house,
Who else has now surpassed
  Quietus with a bare bodkin?
Wind-chimes, far enough off,
  Yet mellower wind-chimes
In the porch we never stopped at,
  Become bells on billygoats,
Nannies too, on a rosemary slope
  Grazing, out of harm's way.

Keyboard

Almost as if it strummed on them
Again that grey bird struts across
The serried bricks that crown a wall:

One arpeggio and away he flits.
Abuzz with metaphor, earth and air
Agree, bewildering me, almost.

The notes ran on, on and out.
I know, in their succession, tunes
No strut of mine could counterpoint.

Claws, if I should put them in
And drag into the air, now mute,
Still no cadenza from the deep, what then?

This Confidence

Voice of a girl from Tibet,
   how she sang, to tidy gongs,
      her cantilena

audible starlight, I'll open
   the door a crack, tonight
      our animals may freeze,

no, not ours, and shelter here,
   locally, is none, go on
      with you, for now pretend,

ask them in, not scaring
   the skunk, domestic and wild
      alike, we jimbel a bit,

perch, curl up, we fill our skins,
    we listen, we find
        this confidence in breathing.

The Tenor on Horseback

As the tenor on horseback was,
    In mid-aria, carried backstage
And the hurriedly hired circus horse
    Soon reappeared, for the next
Bar of the aria, only to resume his
    Circuitry, so my thought, too seldom now,
Brings back into focus the old reasons given
    For worldly being, for ways
Unspeakable pain might be made sense of.

    Surely they were wise, in their robes of cotton,
And never distracted, those midnight men,
    Those who pondered the laws of creation,
Who saw, behind the rotation of the stars,
    Not nothing at all but love with a design?
Of what now is known they knew little,
    Of where feelings come from, of chemical
Reaction in the brain, of chromosomes,
    They knew not a thing.
Yet spelling it out, time the fugitive,
    Vanity liquidating every place desired,
Memory doomed as an ostrich gobbling,
    Instead of water, stray bullets,
Hadn't they told it like it was?

    Yes. There is *kellipot*, the shattering:
Something began, but pulverised its vessels:
    They could not contain the tremendous ray
Shot from the head of En-Sof, alias Adam Kadmon,
    And the task of reconstitution, writ,
Writ it is in holy books, no poppycock.

Even then I wonder if, much as they meant
Well and told of truth as they surprised her,
    It was authority alone that they pursued –
Mobile men on camel or horseback,
    Some next to naked, observing the buffalo,
Dared to command the rough and the tumble,
    Mind's bow measuring its pitch of tension,
Then letting fly its projectile power.

    Privy to secret tunes, vibration
Fathomless in a supposedly divine
    Cosmogonic harp, whose tonalities
Happened as heaven and haunted as riffs
    The blood of us who ache in the pit,
Surely their pursuits refined the liberty to question:
    They combed great glowing spaces for fresh disbelief.

    Job, in the stories told of him, was he confident
Of working a change in Jehovah's attitude?
    Of peeling away an immutable mask? In true tales
Of justice, hollow model and stale god dissolve:
    Creations, subjecting their creators to change,
Gather around them present pain, to relieve,
    A little, sour delusions fixing the scowl or grin.
Slowly, unperceived, a new design will enter
    These mutant mobile geometries of species, hurting –
Or else, for want of variation, all is dispersed.
    Agony abides, look, listen, even if people,
People change, and smile.

            Expressionless the Vast:
To fly in its face, to contradict it, midnight men
    Composed imagination; each, his manifold
Travelling deep design, soul to the cut stone,
    He grounded in earth, sidereal or not;
And as a mason scoops, then trims the mortar,
    He toils with time and the blade of his trowel.

Metapontum: The Necropolis

Come the Spring
Doves moan again
With new warmth

★

Dull I was
It was age
So I thought

Heaven help the young
Now ten feet up
I crash around town

★

Lips part to speak
I spread my wings
Take that perfect wife
This jack-rabbit jumps

[Lucanian red-figured lebes gamikos, Pantanello, Tomb 354]

Saying Goodnight to Kate

Red wine, pink salmon,
Green beans with butter:

Will she at twenty speak
Thriftily? We eat, drink.

Of any discourse you please
Fill out the sphere, Kate!

Pictures you bring, cut
In stone, printed:

Ostrich eye detail, delicate
Hand, over fold of dress

Fingers flexing. Mango
Ice, raspberries follow –

Our feast, on second thought,
Of king fools. Then what's that

Scream, sudden, unearthly,
Almost on the doorstep,

Primal rage? You estimate:
Schoolgirl, pleased exam is over.

Down stair you go,
Loaned umbrella springs open,

Smell of rain, first a whisper –
While, speaking out

Nine centuries gone, I hear
Lu Yu, diehard, crusty soldier

By bigwigs also shafted
(Though mostly mum

As to grits he ate) –
Came serenely over me:

Wild rain, then shock –
'On edge of want, whole lifetime …'

Ragtag Tartar sneers, China fawning.

Outlive Cordelia, Kate.

The First Portrait

Then she went and died on us,
Just like that. And her face, extinct.
We saw nothing move in it, trouble it,
Or rest content, or yawn, or give her smile,
Or even scowl, for us to laugh at.

★

Then we watched while the knife man
Cut off her head. We watched
And took out our loudest voices,
And twisted them in hoots, yelps,
Groaning as the scoop went in;
Spring water washed away the gunk;
Till that was done we howled.

★

Then came the woman with her clay
And stuffed the skull with it,
And made her face again, the face
We could not bear to never see.

★

A clay face for her, any moment now
See its motions; so for her alone
We copied, breathless, the big silence.

★

But to give her all the credit,
Body and head we buried together.
Her clay face had to belong down there.
Our underground is memory of her,
For her the memory is part of us
Who anyway forget. How else
To undo our division?

★

Gossips will say an ostrich
Invented such a funeral custom.
We hope her clay-featured egg,
Not popping so its eyes of sea-shell,
Will hatch and she return to us,
Or with her glance encourage others,
Good kin, who drink at Jericho
The waters of our spring.

(Note: A skull with the face modelled in clay [Natufian, Proto-Neolithic, c. B.C.7500] was excavated at Jericho. See Grahame Clark, World Prehistory: An Outline, *1962.)*

Orbiana

I could never help uttering a light soupir,
Just one, whenever the times
Were hard; today
Just one more, it hardly passed my lips,
But murdered they were, such news,
Murdered near Mayence, those two
Who sent me here, to Leptis Magna.

The emperor was never up to it, really,
In peace or war. She governed, Julia Mamaea,
Selecting me for him. So when she found,
To her astonishment, that I, a tiddler,
Had it in me to influence Alexander,
She packed me off, with his consent –
Nobody knew where. Nobody, either, now
Will inquire where I come from, nobody
Will know which city in Africa
Took me in, so I have disappeared.

But the shopping is quite splendid.
In this great new city of arcades,
Several temples to various divinities,
A triumphant arch, the amphitheatre
And almost superfluous fortifications,
There are nice people to listen to
And black weavers who manufacture
Singular objects to recline or to stand on.

Yes, for the Christians Mother had a soft spot;
From Syria once she had a cavalry escort sent
To save that tyke, whatever his name was.
It starts like mine with O and R.

I like to beachcomb. It attracts,
Ha ha, I mean the beach attracts provincials.
And yet, and yet… From Rome
And from Pamphylia come
Real artists with guitars, who chant
Devotedly of ocean, even to the moon –
I never had children, what a shame,
And the years of loving, few, complicated
By Mother, them I've forgotten now.
The shopping gets, by the way, a bit
Monotonous. Funds I was allowed
Exhaust themselves, somehow,
Even though I did, if I remember rightly,
Stir up a nasty fracas, insist
On statutory imperial support.

I feel behoved to say (don't ever quote me
On this) that I am not yet negligible,
Negligible enough to mark the passage
From finite to infinite. I was not one to wheedle,
But those officiants, what rot they talk –
Into the atoms they ship their designated
Sacrifices, not into some dock of heaven.
Where bodies tasted chance, they make a waste.

You should see me glimpse, now and then,
Into the shrinking bijou bag under my bed.
The wind cooling profuse vegetation
And the display of stars at nightfall
Are supposed to console. They don't.
Disease, at least, is hereabouts minimal.
What a mercy my destination was not Mauretania.
That's such a long, long way west.
And Mauretanians, they do say,
Are a scruffy lot. Please write
To your little friend, Orbiana.

The Aquinas Anecdote

Most unsettling:
How light picks naturally
On such prominences –
The puddle, the muttonbone,
Rufous leaf, and jellies.

Does it want
A surface to stand on? Glide over?
Huge facts attract
My mind, a flick of the sun
Baffles it, like light itself
It wants at least a leaping
Frog skin to settle on. In God's name,
What then is want?

On a frog's intestine picks
A dark, for certain. Gripped
By feuding demon families does intellect
Stoop dejected, does it?

We'll turn that entire construct
Around, turn it

According to the very reasons
Adduced by those philosophers:

                    No redundance,
There can be no redundance in the One
Gradual Lord I know evolves
By variegated replication –

And 'his delight is with the sons of men.'
So evils, wait, evils opt for vacancy, when,
Stopping thought, presumptuous *will*
Projects it on an emptied glass:

The real is fruitful to the brim.
Now pass the decanter, if you please

AND THAT WILL SETTLE THE MANICHEES

Roared huge Thomas d'Aquino, thumping
A fist so beefily upon the table –
Surprising, for till then had come
From his lips not a murmur.
They say the King of France
Then beckoned to his secretary,

Whose eye pursued the pointing finger:
Over there? On your tablet
(It was aggrieved, the royal conscience)
Note that friar's illumination, pronto.

Pseudo-Paracelsus

Cedar seeds, spores of forest
Look like scum, tiny rafts;
Swim among them, and dry,
Dry as gold, thirty-seven ovals,
The fallen leaves of oak,
They float, involved
With skin you wear, with scum.

Holy Moses, on a second look
The spores are tiny spider people,
Tiny drowned spider people;
Are castaways in water,
With arms and legs spread out;
Impotent, captive in a colossal
Aquatic orbit freshening the pool.

Unaccountable, savage, and generous
Excess of nature, so you flood space,
Nothing is nondescript in it. Quick,
I'll hurry home, tidy up
My fly's perch on the surge's tip,
Where, curiously, time is bliss
And I can calculate some more.

Imagine Mallarmé

Imagine Mallarmé with a long and vaporous
Periphrasis buttonholing, at his desk, the mayor
Of Mézy-sur-Seine in 1890, imploring him
To rid the neighbourhood of a herd of pigs,
Which he politely called, of course, *messieurs*.

The matter bothered for a while, at least,
Eugène Manet and Berthe Morisot.
They loved the summer house they'd rented,
But rainy days and then the pig noise
And pig smell from a neighbour's yard

Reduced their pleasure and her chance to paint.
Meanwhile, from Giverny, not far away,
Monet wrote: *My canvases, I ruin them,*
Scraping out whatever I've accomplished.
What I achieve is beneath anything.

The Manets and Mallarmé in a carriole
Took off to visit Monet in Giverny.
After lunch, on Sunday, July 13, 1890,
Monet, to compensate for having failed
To do for Mallarmé a promised illustration,

Told the poet to take a picture home.
Mallarmé didn't dare to choose the one
He liked the most, but soon, persuaded
By Berthe herself to take it, he did so.
Then going home to where the pigs were stinking,

Oink oink in the distance, Mallarmé declared,
His painting luminous across his knees
While the carriole jogged through the twilight:
It makes me happy, just to think now
I'm living in the same age as Monet.

Chekhov at Sumy

First to go, the right lung;
Then, at intervals, unanticipated
Spates of spitting blood.

Devotedly at work, the iridescent
Stories; unhopeful
'Doctoring in my spare time;'
Focus on fact, on detail, all those letters.

1890: by boat the long haul to Sakhalin,
The prison swamps, and duly eye-opening
His report. Somewhere else
He builds a school, takes charge

Of a cholera outbreak. Kropotkin
Quotes his dictum with approval:
We need desire most, force of character
To banish 'whining shapelessness.'

Nightingales had nested in the open window
At Sumy, Summer 1888. While he slept,
One lung, or both, might have whistled
So entertainingly, the light-winged
Dryad of the woods joined in.

Not a remnant, left to erode
In acidic debate,
He purposed and accomplished
The utmost he had known –

Sixteen more years above the dust.
In two, from Ukleyevo, Lipa, Lipa,
Her baby scalded, and her scream
Building,

Complete as now his pleasure is
To see 'slip from their shells
The children of the nightingale.'

Chekhov in a Park

The pince-nez; above it,
Shadowing nothing at all,
His hat, new, with a wide brim,

Had it poured the rest of him out?
He's well and truly here:
Anton, the uninvented.

No tricks. On a rickety
Park bench, somewhere south,
Nonchalantly Anton sits.

He crossed his long thin legs.
He had polished his boots.
He manages to be elegant.

Unmistakeably the gentleman,
They say, he was in touch,
Not love, with everything:

Worse, he winnowed,
Out of marshy claptrap, through
This one visible ear,

His translucent mountain –
Psyche, likewise, from the Styx
Drew a crystal bottle.

Anton filtered chat, not only
To select, but chisel
Nugget after nugget,

Capture from somnolent liquids
An articulated fabric:
Many unstable dimensions,

Much heartache. Out of copper,
Antimony, tin, others made
Mugs of pewter. Anton's ear,

Here it shows, in the photo,
Made trouble – some
People, sinking, wilt, by struggle

Blasted. At work
In this vertical head
Something was dependable:

Plumb, his touch went up,
A spiral, into sorrow,
Down deep inside, inside

Even happiness. And peering
From the sleeve, so small,
So curly, like a claw, a hand.

Judge Bean

> *Of him or her who placed it there, and why,*
> *No one knew anything.*
> Thomas Hardy

Judge Roy Bean of Long Ago
Beheld once in a magazine
The face of Lily Langtry,
And in the twilight often
Judge Bean upon his porch
Rocked in a rocking chair,
Upon his porch he'd rock,
And dream and dream of her.

A distant blue, how it pulls
The flesh to Long Ago
And far away, although
Judge Bean had hopes:
Lily Langtry just might come,
Passing through, and sing to him.

Not far from where the judge
Had sat and rocked and hoped
There was a tree festooned
With bottles that were blue.
Over the tips of many twigs
Somebody had been slotting
Milk of Magnesia (Phillips),
His empties, by the dozen.

Well-water there is hard;
Deep canyons through the rock
The Rio Grande, a trickle now,
Had had long since to carve.
There too the mountains host
Various flocks of birds,
Yet not a one would choose
To nest in such a tree.

The tree, so dead its twigs
That pronged the bottles, have
They in the meantime broke?
A striking sight against the sky,
An image not to be forgot,
So many bottles of blue glass
And sips of milk drunk up,
It still explodes to mark
Dimensions in the mind,
A horizon in the heart.

Long before the twigs had pronged
Blue bottles for my sight,
Like Tao it had for sure
No name at all, that place

Where Judge Bean rocked;
But Lily Langtry's face
Nothing airy in his mind,
Not despairing of his dream,
One stormy day he took his pen
And wrote:

Now Langtry is its name.

Felo de se

When he had pulled upright his jingle-jangle cart,
he said he hoped he would not be disturbing me.
He unpacked his kit from the cart and lost no time
but baited his lines with worms from a box of dirt
and made a long cast for the lead to plop in mid-river.

When he says he is Tex-Mex but spoke as a child
no Spanish, he explains that he took himself soon
to school, learning the way they speak it in Spain.

When he was little his father died, says he.
So he helped in the house, cleaning and sweeping,
cooking the beans, washing dishes for mother.

When he had a family of his own, two boys
and a girl, he told them, one by one, as they grew,
there'll be no lazy nobodies in my house,
told them when it was time to grow up
and that it won't be easy but here's your support,
grow up to be somebody with an education:

Now there's my boy in the marines (this war, it makes
no sense) but then his line is aviation, the mechanics,
in law-school the girl, the other boy in medicine,
and all three speak Spanish as well as they do English.

When he's set to make a cast with his third rod,
he says his father-in-law's funeral cost ten thousand,
but his own uncle's was cheaper for he was cremated.

And when he has cast with a fourth rod far out
into mid-river, he says that he'll be tonight
in Marble Falls where the catfish bite better,
that because of the funeral he has a week off.

But when he went to Mexico he didn't like it,
didn't like the Mexicans, a crooked lying crowd,
says he, they look down on us, call me a gringo.

Me, I'm a carpenter, he says, I can build you
a pretty house, restore, where wood has gone to rot,
repair, adapt, install any kind of cabinet:

anything to do with wood, I can do it with finish,
fishing is just a pastime when you're needing it,
and it has clouded over now, the fish like that.

Yes, he says, any kind of wood, I can handle it,
and we were standing under a water-cypress,
a very tall tree that has gone brown by March,
the tangle of its roots ran in long looped
cylinders out under water, while he talked,

wearing a cobalt gimme cap with NY in a monogram,
an olive-green tabard (pockets in place of emblems),
drainpipe trousers and spongy-soled suede boots,

yet all I had asked was if he knew perhaps
the meaning of *felo de se*, supposing it Spanish.
Not theft, he said, thieving is *robar, robo;*
what you said, might that be in a book?

Senex

Hearing at night the first Fall Norther
I think no more of Artaud's tantrums;
No more of Ungern-Sternberg's magnificent beast;
Of balance perfect in the form of a pear
I think, then poof it goes, the Buddha temple.

That wall: it is the rock face of a mountain.
Fumbling for a handhold, slowly slowly
I step sideways, the ravine at my heels
Deepens, unsteadily I must step sideways.

Nose to nose with my mountain wall,
The path no wider now than a foot's length,
How will it end, where then shall I go?

I had to limber up, to risk a look:
And what I'd thought was not, was not –
But was a plain, immense, and it was shaping
Soon to become a fair field of folk.
Still it wanted curvature for a horizon,
Still it hid its dells and lakes and alps;
Now in it rose, I see, putting them there,
Many many footholds I had mistaken
For brushes quicker than a breath, contacts
Of clothes in the café, in a shop –
Yet people, singly, clusters, were appearing,
All distinct, each face rich in expression:
Scowling, perplexed, then relief, the smile
Brief or broadening, and grim if in revenge.

Every single glance grew thriftily from the stem,
Unmistakeable, inexchangeable, the body.

And by the balls the horror of it got me:

There was no way to make good
Wrongs of my doing. With one quick breath,
No way, to chuck the humbug; to be done

With dithering; understand at least
A secret dread; so to bring crashing down
As vapour only, absorbed back into earth,
The tabernacle cant, enforced conformity,
Those violations that had shrunk my time,
And to annul in me the predator,
Root out of me the pest, indifference.

Oh well, so much abstract projection
Still is, tooth and nail, a hanging-on.
Symmetry I did perceive, agile in faces,
Stormy, or in suspense, it might promise
Value, though passion rushed, then halted. Stooping
You could glimpse the star, absurd, it was afloat
Where the well-shaft had no end.

Then I was touched.
                              Then I was free.
I turn, how else, alone again, to the mountain.

The Whelk

Today the rain is not a torrent,
For normally the mockingbird
Will sing to celebrate clear light,
And now percussive, rid of any tune,
His song for half an hour has shot
Sparks, astonishing, from his throat:
Still his beak is piping an acerb
Tumult from his lungs.

An empty wineskin comes to seem
What the universe is not –
Piping bird, and in her fingers
The good schoolgirl turns her whelk,
Wondering about it, minding the violence.
Her toes might have buried it:

Now Athena treasures what she found,
Hearing the spark, rain drum down,
On leaves and asphalt, she peers
How curious, into the whelk's throat.

At school she might be wondering still
Who saw sparks patter out of a bird;
How someone knew her name and copied
Her thought about the whelk, its helix.
A centrifuge of rhythms, while it grew
I spelled it out as filaments from spider me:

Here in the gleam that rides a dolphin
Is there a temple, for a god an aviary?
No. They have not wronged Athena yet –
The sylph finds no refuge in a syllable.
Unless for joy invention jumped them,
Cold facts account for her not needing to.

All in good time. Now who hid my shoes?
My satchel? And the laws, Athena thinks,
Who will fairly number, sparkling in the whelk,
Particles which make nature happen – twelve?

(Rebecca Elson, poet-astrophysicist, 1960–99.)

Ancient Emigré (Irish)

Once only I've heard in (of all places)
This candybar town, where songs
Are composed by the dozen, composed
In the beds, on the porches,

A person singing at work. (Ten years back,
Must I recall, I passed on a street
In the outskirts a fellow who sang
For joy, while walking, a popular song.)

Among cabbages, this nineteenth
Of November, 2005, I noted, yes,
Among cabbages, celery, spinach,
Heaps of arugula, vegetables from

Half the world over, a young caballero
Singing, and it was 'Molly Malone'.
Sweeping the floor, fresh-faced he was,
With a daredevil forelock, and as he sang

That song of the streets, some broad,
Some narrow, I pictured rooftops,
Flat rooftops in Corsica, women sing there,
Soon after sunrise, answering songs

Sung by their neighbours, at work
Hanging the laundry out. On broccoli,
Snap beans and cauliflower dwelled
This morning the eyes of shoppers, all

Attentive to tasks having today to be done.
That Molly Malone could have sunk
So deep in the people who pushed their carts
Hither and thither, heaping the produce up,

The shaft of her glance, startled them with
Obstreperous beauty (rough, into the bargain,
From counting the pennies, privation, abuse);
Could they marvel, I ask, at nothing at all?

My cart hummed with its wires, my kilo
Of strawberries trilled, *conamore* the praties,
Onward wheeling the work with a song,
Did it? Briefly. Midnight. Now I inhale

And smell in this paper I scribble on
Molly, her skin. Her wheelbarrow is parked,
My cap's falling off as, friendly-like,
In a bombarded garden, she comes to be mine.

Elegy with Offenbach

The coming century, Dostoevsky said,
Would decide the matter: either Mystery

Or Science was the shape of things to come.
Whichever way you look at it, from 1865

(Or thereabouts) till now, that century
Decided nothing, still the millstones

Grind, still the matter hangs, pulpy,
Or adamant, grit, their justification.

Russians (those were the days) could frame,
On lines drawn up between opposing factions,

Their big ideas, each faction on its axis.
Exclusive orbits, 'Science' or 'Religion,'

Each turned on a dream of time at an end,
Of a new time beginning, when Necessity

Finally throws a switch to snarl the traffic:
Then – holy smoke – the showdown, an Apocalypse.

Offenbach's 'Barcarole,' now I hear it,
A quick waltz in slow time for counterpoint,

Accompanied in the morning our patrol
As tiny children circling the assembly hall:

We did not dance the waltz, we walked it;
We did not know it was a boating song,

But we patrolled, circling the airy room,
And soon we crept into a world constructed

To harsher rituals, helped in our pursuits,
Or butchered, by designs the science fashioned.

Hearing again the music, trite as it is,
A parlour music, anything but the cancan,

Not Shostakovich, and not Babi Yar,
I rise to a dream, and with quaint emotion

Recognise that, all along, inexplicably,
It might have been for me a paradigm.

If it did not show you how to yearn,
If it did not open heart to high heaven,

The music showed the children how to move
Without mishap, synchronise the body

With a tune, to find arithmetic less foreign,
Build on a page of squares the vaults of letters.

Another forty years… Then reflexed cogitation
Towered above a scoop of archaic deposits wavily

Secreted in the individual. Dark tools
Of flint, snowy temples, tinkling doubloons,

Then casks of contradiction, high-minded quips,
Grovelling phobias bled into ginger – those

Were the legal cargo housed in your tug
Or fishing smack, galleon, or destroyer.

No match for commerce few can get a hold on,
The gods, many do say, chucked in the sponge;

What then of atavisms, mutinous in the bilge,
If in the deep itself the sea-girl mocks it all?

Volatile ballast, these and other millstones:
Who calls from the look-out? What think you, captain,

Measuring good and evil when the ship rolls?
What kind of magic matter keeps the hulk afloat?

Pictogram for a Maquisard

Elle voit maigrir les oiseaux inquiets.
René Char

A thought moth,
Incandescence
Hollowing the dark out,
Combusts in the genitive
Metaphor's blur –
How then in hell persists,
Bitterly, brightening, futile,
A breath of air, the word?

Fool, in a tone alone
Lurked the virtue,
And larked, with soul, too,
And ate up the miles,
All the bitter hours:
Remember the king, his corpse
Wrapped in a Book of the Dead,
Rose to walk in the land of On.

Anchored in love of earth,
Skylark, your song
Spirals ever up, transcendent
In itself; so, diffuse, this falling
Squeal of a red-tailed hawk
Echoes to tell its nested young,
I will be homing soon
With perfect flesh for thee.

Election Eve in the Lord's Republic

(in the manner of Jakob van Hoddis, 1911,
as modified by Alfred Lichtenstein)

Bad dogs are wondering where the turtles go;
A misty gloom pervades the park today;
Demure inside their shells the turtles know
What the bad dogs are plotting as they play.

On TV screens a twitchy talking head –
Baseball, sundry bombs, and ads for beers:
'Terrists (*sic*) will capture you in bed.'
A choir of parrots chuckles Four More Years.

Look at the lady jogger on her knees:
What fashionable prayer might she pray?
By rights there should be herons in the trees.
The herons, blue or white, have stalked away.

Their tops are flat, the bell-towers in our town:
Again the gasp of spirit is its last.
Again we let the force of nature down:
The space we violate, the time we waste.

A coot capsizes, croaking for a drink.
Poodles police good dogs who stop to piss.
By now we should have been enlightened, think –
The great-grandfathers never wanted this.

Fear of God ten thousand moons ago:
If speech broke free, the speaker had to fry.
Now God and Terrists co-produce the show,
Baboon stars with Flapdoodle in full cry.

A water-skier splashed into the lake.
Some nasty weather blew up from the West.
Bad dogs made off with someone's birthday cake.
The turtles do not answer when addressed.

33

Against Frenzy

Hail bright spirit and bony
Fingers in a backyard shifting
To pick strings, few to dwell on,
And local voices, hail,
Uncouth you crow to keep a slow tune turning.

Only the other day a prophetess alleged
That justice flees
From the field of the victorious;
Astronomers, that the universe is beige –
It is the dust, if any settles
On a book, on the back
Of tympanum and monolith.

In a singlet costumed, sailor pants,
Elvis of tennis, the baboon Nadal
Has fired off a winning shot and whirls,
Exhibiting his muscled butt, punching up through air
A phallic fist. My, see his prance,
When millions roar, watching him hit

With malice, bodily, this it is
Degrades his art, in ostentation of it,
Degrades his public, now vomiting applause –
Over and again you hear the rasp in it
Of a gladiator's eyeballs rolling.

Do they love him? Not a bit.
So the dust of soldiers' bones,
So justice never done to mothers, each
Met with indifference, making oblivion gross,
Are no talk of the neighbourhood.

That much more vivid, a song is almost
The midway thing I snootily imagine.
A shattered god three chords compose
Has been repatriated. Quiet now.
Emerald. Turquoise. Rose.

A Paper Snake

All along, the snake of concentrated paper
Drooped from a branch of the plum tree.
His eyes measuring the little tree in its tub
Had eliminated the balcony.
Now he was discovering it afresh. The snake
Was moving, its wedge of a head
Knocked on the tree's always thickening stem;
It plipped and perked up, as leaves do
When rain of a late summer afternoon
Breathes on the tree, or gives it a soak.
Black, yellow, and red, distinctly
The sections of the snake were arching over
Remote rectangular city blocks.
Offices there, hoisted flags, the apartment house.
Remote, he said, and mind you stay that way.
Your comforts disappoint or spoil me,
Wiggle I will, free of materiality's headlock.
I repulse the busybodies who haunt
Your mass, your pressure, your crises:
I'll not suck hind tit on that body no more.
This book now, concerning chromosomes,
That's what I want, for wonder I do
How profoundly robotic a lot of behaviour is.
But the snake's the limit. *No pasaran.* Duchesne
On early histories of the church holds me
Fascinated today; I open it, there, and fumigate
My cave. That was all he said, the artist.
I should confute his aversion, but how?
He leers out of his echoing catacomb;
He points like an idiot, jaw propped on fist,
For me to see he points
At a paper snake.

The Wine Merchant's Secret

Only in mid-
November from the trumpet vine
Pods fall.

The fall I do not hear, only
A pitterpat
When they hit the tarmac.

I should hear the tacit
Rush of air around them seething
As they drop; a loud

Pop as they break loose
From what it is that holds them,
In secret, to the stem.

Also I should admire
A monstrous waste. Iniquities,
Our own, despoil the shining

Earth, suck
Her abundance out, pump through
Crooked markets her antique excess.

Another knock. I thought
Of thieves.
There are species

Of salesmen who do not look up
In hotel breakfast rooms
Now to say hello.

They have an air of spies. The pods
Are barren. Yet vines
Proliferate, so picturesque,

Mornings, across the sunny
Window pane they blot so tangible,
I must resist

Temptation, before I cook,
On my fingertip to feel
My jugular in their pulse.

The Incident

Worried child, whose tiny fingers
Stole into mine that day
Your mother ran, all knee and elbow,
Out into the market parking lot

With good reason, even if you could not
Possibly fathom it – a helicopter
Roared from a roof, and she had
Slammed a hand on the hood

Of a pick-up pulling in reverse away –
Even if no bullet smashed the glass
Door we stood at, only looking on,
For no advantage ever forfeit

The trust your hand put into mine,
Warm with your being, while uneasily
Independent, there, by me you stood
Firm in your small shoes, not losing blood.

But of waifs by the million,
Every which way swivelling bright their eyes,
City brats nowhere at home in the squalor,
Child, our gesture salvaged not a one.

Whatever Moves

In the huge new Museum of Free Will
Make straight for the saints and the monsters.

If that's where the crowd is thickest
And your precious time need not be wasted

On scales and degrees that distinguish exhibits
In the Congo Gallery or Seminar Hiroshima,

Spare a moment for the average savvy bloke.
He is portrayed as old Mr Fixit.

It is explained that he never took
(As Fortune's plaything, of course)

A complete reckoning of his fears,
Never fathomed them to the root of their

First surge or up and up to where, who knows –
Since intimately examined they were not.

Yet what a wonderful way he has with him.
All those things he did for us and still does

Are to his credit listed in his cubicle,
Where, if you push a button, the dummy does an act.

Now whatever he sees move helps Mr Fixit
Get out of bed and walk. Whatever moves

Promises him arrival at the perfection
To which his savvy never found the way.

There's a dead calm, afternoons in summer;
He likes the way it reforms round the gurgle

Of a car passing or flavours in a soup.
But best he likes the purple and vermilion.

Of colour, even, even if it moves,
Touching his mind, he's not afraid at all.

What must he not have seen besides
Cities becoming rubble, and the poor

Ramshackling through but never out
Of darkness, stench, and being tyrannised,

That he remembers of it just a little?
Whatever moves, he'll take it in his stride.

The Wind-Chimes

Trite as ever these chimes hang
   From a hook in the wind.
Rusted, sun face with a mouth
   In the shape of an almond –
Neither grinning nor grim.

Discarded during redecoration
   Of a home below, rusty thing
Outstaring emptiness,
   I lifted it up, recycled
A radiant artifact of old metal.

So much rusted it emits now
   No chime. Eight little bells,
Tongues in no hurry to speak;
   Wheel stuck clockwise, asking
Our hurricane to quit.

Small Change, AD 147–8

Small change in its time, the bronze
Dupondius, and in fair shape still,
Touching its round the ball of a thumb
Responds to the relief elevating a head.
That emperor flourishing it
Brought peace with him.

                Reverse the coin,
And here Britannia crouches,
Worn flatter, supposedly
On a rock (a cloud, more like);
Elbow on thigh she lifts
Toward her lips a forefinger.

               You can hardly spare
A moment, to find your own, shimmering,
In the slow stream of clothes, beliefs, and faces.
Merry hell they played with certain signs, the mix
And mass of sedulous peoples; blinded by event
We did let slip away some fragile, airy good.

              Indeterminate sea
Our share and breathing it
With names for the twenty sea-winds,
Still we transport our space, no escaping it:

             A plough behind her
Could be a longboat's tiller. To it
Her left hand is put. She'll be thinking up,
Surely, ways to muddle on through,
And in the Great Memory to cradle
Old birds who bled to death for you.

The Brink

Air crisp,
  Sky bright – at long last
On a day like this
  You come to life again.

    On a winter day like this,
Nine strikes: remember
  Gilgamesh. To your disbelief
You might see forever.

    Then such a silence.
Not the hush wrenching the heart.
    Not a mousehole, either,
To humble, one by one, the bones.

    Stories: catch a first
Whiff of stories to be told.
Those inventions
    Of a posterity uncrushed,

Hear them truly,
  Just as soon as that
Posterity will have been invented.

Homily with Reeds

Noticed before but not seen
And still not seen
Deeply in the round,
The dozen or so
Vertical reeds – fuzzy and tall
Tubular caps they have on;
At angles they grow but
Straight; and sway they do,
Absurdly, in the wind.

And that self you never knew
For shallow, in the round,
Drives impervious on
Over the bridge they grow beside,
Up the sunken
Road that split, long ago,
For your pursuit
Somewhere else,
Their stone background.

Pascal, probing as it was,
Your mathematical remark
That 'man is a thinking reed'
Still fails to thaw,
In its tracks, an icily
Expanding spirit. Or blowing hot
His murderous traffic thickens;
Consumed, his huts of reed;
His ashen towers drink the starlight up.

Marginalia

The Third Man Reconsidered

When with his valise and crumpled face
The hero struts to the desk of his hotel,

Who might in 1945 predict the celluloid of events?
Had they quit Vienna, all the Catholic Nazis?

Will winter never cease, will the Soviets,
Jittery in a Zone, help a little bit?

The Shylock lookalike shuffles with high helium
Balloons bubbling above his head. He'll traverse

The plaza as a shadow. Shylock himself is squat
And at a portal wheedles to the hidden khaki

Cockney cop – Buy One? Buy One? (Sergeant,
How could you not blink at his deathcamp smell?)

Yet, dismal as there, particular events
Unroll crisscross on slick nocturnal streets;

Through the cloaca cameras drag uglier shades
Of hope, manhole-covers pop, clatter shut, the girl,

The girl steps into a cold train, the parrot
Bit the hero's finger, not the trigger one,

And all mixed up he runs the other way. No less
A barnacle in the nautilus of a stairwell,

Clotho tattily sheathed in her eiderdown,
The widow protests Mine is a Decent House.

For the concierge received a tiny bullet,
The schoolboy screamed It's Him, gives chase

But not behind the bad guy. No, cabined inside
The Wheel he keeps (ah, Fortune what a slow

Vast revolving matter you do provide for futile
Conversation) a rendezvous, and out the evil comes.

Meanwhile, hush, for the brain-dead children
Line up, invisible, in cots. The ward is dim,

Yet pinpointed for an instant, unhugged,
A teddybear has not a soul to talk to.

Who did for the babies? The bad guy, of course.
Footsteps of the nun beside the bear

Are slowed by a huge contraption, like
A ship for an elf, sequestering her skull.

Enough, the climax. Plunge into the cloaca,
And fancy that, for Orson, rotten

From ravening after scandal, thrills, power,
His fingers in the grille, if I got his nod

I'd shoot him in the back, like Joseph Cotten did.
Then, presto, a funeral. Between parallel trees

Saunters the girl, sunk under her immutable hat
(She never did betray him, or did she?).

Not batting an eyelid, she'll pass the hero up;
She takes her time, dissolves right into us.

A Demon Sniggering

'Poetry,' said a voice, 'should not
Do philosophy.' What withering Platonism

Was this? Or, hawked by a shrunken pundit,
A neat political scheme? Of itself,

Utterly other than propositional discourse
(Mimetic maybe, but memory's instance

Leaving 'a snail's trail of grass-halms bent
Darker against the dew'), poetry bleeds,

And some of it brands (in its veins philosophical
Fire) thought that 'ordains what abides.'

The codes converge, the codes,
At times they miscegenate, as gods

Come alive in a freshness haunting
Hope, in unharmful belief.

They do seek it out, in the citizen –
Freshness, to ventilate

Atavisms, change them into
Productions, of justice, of the good.

Your Aeschylus gave Athena this to do.
Then one by one the furious

Eumenides, at her philosophising well,
Freshened, into food. Freshly yet,

Voice, you did so turn the words
As to discern, in their penumbra,

A demon sniggering too,
As facts, turned ugly, speak true.

[On reading Anna Moschovakis' poem 'Six Nights.']

A Happy Captain

On holiday blue Manet painted a steamboat,
Flecks of colour – trippers; from a funnel
Sang a wisp of fume – was that a hoot?
Departure certainly excites the pulses
Of any individual and brisk brush-stroke.

Because, two centimeters tall, a captain
Posed on the bridge, Commander Pontillon
Refused the picture offered as a gift.
The giver, sister-in-law to the Commander,
Herself a painter, Manet's brother's wife,

Could judge when Manet got a detail wrong
Or set a scene to beggar belief. However,
Strictly Navy, the Commander couldn't.
For him, no painting, thank you, with a real fault:
Look, on the bridge, the captain, at departure?

Ça, voyez-vous, çe ne va pas du tout!
Nonchalant, valid as an amulet the captain
Posed, having the passengers at heart,
Carefree, so to secure their confidence,
Was that it, Manet? An icon for the bourgeois,

A red memorial to their holidays?
And not yet visible there inside it
The first mate at the helm, already
By his boots betrayed, now shedding his disguise –
Out he will strut, the wonderful dictator.

Bouillons

The Apple

When I halve the apple
Faces that appear
Give me an honest look.

When I halve the half,
Round a corner, slyboots,
Who are you peeking at?

Shoelaces

When my Paulina, feeling hot,
Has spread her limbs and sighed,

How come you snarl into a knot
Which cannot be untied,

Yet on my lone patrols abroad
You snap
Or loosen of your own accord?

White-Out

Typed words lie killed in action,
Never quite deleted
By a liquid swansdown,
For smear they do their origin
And wrong its ingenuity.

Paperclips

Anything to go one up
On those French
Who call you trombones,
I will invent the Greek
And call you hippodromes

Evoking on the instant
Greens and Blues
And the furious races
The riots and revolutions
Triumph and torment
When Constantinople was Ours.

Cowslips

are not negroid but to quote
Alfred Russel Wallace's account
of Darwin on the topic –
    the insect has to take
pollen from the interlabial
stamen of the one variety
and leave it on the stigma
of the other with its stamen sheltered
halfway down the petal tube

and thus occurs 'most surely' by
cross-pollination high fertility –
Off and on for seventy years
your trumpets elfin yellow blown
across a meadow and their scent
no less precisely I recall.

Postcard from William Cowper

To you, good friend, I will confide
(Pray let my theme enjoy approval)
The secret I have sought and found:
Neither rectangular nor round,
The Everlasting must be oval.
Who fails to hatch, him woe betide.

Respond, if this you deem a blooper.
Affectionately, William Cowper.

A Fly

Like laying eggs in spoiled meat,
Like drinking from a starveling's eye,

Savage tricks other kinds get up to,
Thus to oblige their Lord of Counterfeit;

House fly, you are so artful a fly poem
Might set you free from that there windowpane.

Of Adverse Atmospheres

That of those, like mammoth,
   That of a fugitive whiff,
That a thin cloud cover
   Burned off by sunlight,
Was I thinking aloud,
   Thinking at all at all?

Not everything comes back,
   Not many bones are rescued,
Russian a thin man toothless
   Mumbling food poison,
Me only an equal shall murder,
   Filth in a camp far north:

And will sixty-seven years
   Today have passed? That
Of the mammoth bones
   Numbers are dug up,
But his are not –
   Was this another needling
Springtime? Uneasy
   Reminiscence, of modular
Cubes cut, peat, of
   The smoky pinewood?

Shall we try again to catch up
   With Mandelstam?
Secure, perfuming (that
   Again Athena might
Convert the Furies)
   From crypt to pinnacle
His tempestuous work,
   At daily tasks a civil spirit

Must fly into a rage,
   Rage at this harpy
Whose name is national,

Anchoring radio talk
Out of Washington, she
    Balked at his,
Asked Who Was That?

Then on she goes, glib,
    To babble twice
Of Meister Ikehart,
    Meister Ikehart.

From the Cat

The niyam woe is westergone,
The slavit with a shrill,
Betone the ghast, obese the lid,
Alack the cock until.

Crumb forks to pick a winsome up,
One plays the yoick, and then
Another dove into the first,
Or snubs a gentlemen.

You think a looky star will strike,
A wolverine will spin?
Pot nest you snugly, Mister Toph,
But critter risk a grin.

Then if he chews to blow a scowl
Much bitter oft you be –
Since revoluzzers busted ope,
Wobbly the One-in-Three.

Full up your gourd, swot wide away
The chumps that bite behind,
For on the muse left at your door
Red meat you still may find.

Exile

(from the French of Léon-Paul Fargue)

Returned, a nymph, into
   red autumn salt,
     a chrysalis glittered
in hot froth, in smoke
   of a town. Still a town,
     portraits of resin
        gaze through its fabric:
ant-eater, sun-guzzler,
   honey its object, battles
      a moth of iron cutting
a furrow through the sky.

★

Fire in the kitchen
   tinkles. Man gets a laugh
     from doll. Headlight probes
shadow, shoving that clochard
   back. Time was, I stopped,
     dusk coming on, deep summer –

There in a doorway, sans door.
   Immense courtyards, for drink –
     with quick steps, wrong ideas,
in ungentrified boutiques I drank,
   vague venomous things I called,
     with a shiver, by name.

At a door boarded-up, one night,
   music beyond it,
   I stopped. Heart
beat quicker, I had jumped
   into the detour, for safety,
     barely hid a secret
shone there. Then squatting

cross-legged the tailor I saw,
   his shadow
at the end of the corridor.

★

Crows fluttering
   choke a suburban station.
A gate beats its drum

And a smell of rotten egg
   quizzes it, quizzes the freight
scales, the cemetery under them,

Under their tilted
   eye, where, into her shawl,
the newspaper woman wept for her son.

★

That breathing cave
   I drank, of locomotives dozing,
dozing while they shunt,

while the night groans
   and drizzles flies into the furrow
of grease. Like them

My calvary I trundle
   on, like them arrive
at the Chapel. Between the lines

of the sick I take a position;
   I do
just as my companions have done.

★

Come back and save your starveling!
　　With your absent eyes
he weeps. Speak, deep in your pool,

Or tell if the top of the sky
　　still is made
of earth, just a scrap of it:

I'm little, you're big. That's all.
　　Your ideas I adopt,
and know that misery, mine,

derives from desires I had. Look,
　　I'm calm, and I hope.
Help me to shed this visible form.

I'll climb, up the ladders, all.
　　Ordeals and injuries
I'll traverse, and systems

Proliferating from the sun –
　　incubus I am, drop of the fire,
a drop of mud I am. I endure,
　　　　　to know you, such a thirst as mine.

★

Tender, severe, your phantoms
　　haunt my life, dream of a dream.

In the self-deafening town,
　　in a fruit full of earwigs I stand:

I face a wall, to watch, pictured,
　　the contest: Who is Next to Die?

In ramified mind, whacked by the word,
　　in hog-wallow, algae

Naked I strip, naked
   Love's marl.

★

What battering am I plunged into:
   the salvo of ocean guns
      brings news I catch, on the confusion
in my heart, intercepting it.

That injustice, yours, I need that:
   for want of it, of you,
I am the next best thing to a man unknown,

Hair dank, stuck to a brow
   of blue lead, dead
on an alien shore, gathering round him

a crowd, his face by no-one understood.

[Paris, c.1943]

[L.-P.F., 1876–1947]

55

In Memory of W.G. Sebald

A bipolarity remark, native to the species.
Observe ecstasy in acts of laying waste.
Consider your apprehensions at the sight
Of a bone pulled out of an avalanche.
How ecstasy and apprehension skip, consider
Next, the supervision of intellect.

A noise not stopping, very loud, destruction:
Heed the skeleton's poise – as if to speak.
Amnesia, aphasia, anaesthesia remark:
While fleets of souls, all twittering, take off,
A blank occupies pained heart, or vandal head.
One who came through, clutching a god –
Contemplate the god who took away his speech.

Thorny species, a Kalahari shrub,
Shrunk by heat at day's end, contrives
Nocturnally to unwind, seasonally to sprout.
As if that sound were what a desert listens for,
Heed, during a breath or two of cool at night,
The rustle when a thorn, a lucky leaf, expands.

There'll be prognoses printed out, decades in advance
And on a scale so vast that guesswork is eliminated;
Surely with some device we'll temper any rising heat;
Banish the blank from this heart or that head;
Bury the hatchets, for people of tomorrow
Cultivate sensibly earth, all the nursed grudges
Volatilised behold, reformed into the rose
We give to those whom fear set free to think.

Poems 2006–2009

The Enjoyment of Shouting

Artist Unknown

While Tartar advance-guards
tore the settlements apart,
platoons on horseback fanning out,
ugly men, often drunken
torching the huts
with speed and arrow frightening
the tidy inhabitants,
he stayed at home
all bamboo perhaps
and with a steadier hand than once
painted his unforgettable 'Cat
Threatening Butterflies.'

The Dance Itself

What could he have been sniffing at,
This red dog like a retired greyhound
In Gauguin's picture? An enigmatic wave
Runs down his backbone, then up
It goes to the shoulders, those
Of two women, one of them whispering,
One in a dusty blue, the other in white,
Cross-legged, putting a hand on her ankle.

And what could they, posing side by side,
Be communicating? One in profile
Has told the other, in white, of troubles
Perhaps, yet the other looks out at you
Straight-on; surely she has often heard
This sort of little sylvan history?

Behind them, a hard green. Three
Female figures whirl in a dance there.
Our couple sits beneath a tree.
The dog was passing by, in a moment
Off he walked, having doubtless
Dramas of his own to be taking care of.

Might not the eyes then have it to be
That in the picture its principal figures
Articulate one wave, its rise
In the sniffing, its crest in the dancing
At the apex, its fall for the time being
In the whispering? And that this,
Here, is an image of time caught,
Caught by the tail, made by colours
To open itself, become transparent?

At what the dog sniffs we only know
That in no time at all he'll piss on it;
Of what the one woman whispers to the other
We cannot so much as guess, truth to tell;
And what are the distant dancers dancing about,
If not, to rhythms inaudible, the dance itself?

(*Arearea*, 1892)

The Strategy of Apanea

(B.C. 140)

Of the Syrian Greeks it has been reported
That for those who lived in considerable cities
Earth, more or less of her own accord, delivered
All the food and drink they could possibly want.
All day in halls at the long tables carousing,
Or strolling in cool porticos,

While a few slaves distributed nature's productions,
The citizens could pass their time watching shows,
Learning to play the harp, to tell stories.
The city air was filled with eloquence and music,
Flute girls or boys ran up obligingly,
If in a figured bowl you brought your dinner home.

It is also said that the men of Larissa never stopped
Being manly. Ten generations of fighting
From Babylon to the Hellespont
Had not made them think twice about belligerence.
On the march to war with them
Once a brigade of Apameans was discovered.
The hats they flaunted had the broadest brims
And were 'exquisitely adjusted
To shade the neck but not divert the breeze.'
A string of asses trotted behind the Apameans
Laden with wine and every sort of viand;
Pipes and flutes bristled from other baskets –
Instruments (as Posidonius helpfully
Reminds us) not of war but of revelry.

Among Egyptian Cenobites

(Valley of Nitria)

Makarios the Alexandrian in his cave –
A hyena surprised him, holding a little one
Between her teeth. Gently then
She laid it on the rock, at the hermit's feet.
Mother Hyena, she backed off and waited.
Makarios waited too, And soon
He did something.

Blind no more, wisely beside the mother,
Stumbling a bit, off goes the little one.
Days pass. The mother eventually
Revisited the cave, between her teeth
A sheepskin.

When he chose to sleep
Makarios could curl up on it. At a great age
He gave it to the dauntless Roman lady
Melania. She took it home, quite likely,
And tacked it, unlaundered, to the wall.

But if she took the time to scrutinise it,
Melania trembled. Might a hyena's breath
On embers in her memory blow away
Five centuries to Jason,
The Golden Fleece, and the Argonautica
Of Apollonius of Rhodes?

                              To be left behind,
Yawned at? ... Again the lady trembled.
The cave is where it was. Fleece in hand,
And long ago Melania went to heaven.

A Longer Wind

Don't I know well enough how the world turns,
Yet a May morning, this one, prompts me
Less to question the weight of certain sympathies
Than to memorialise a sprinkle of events.

Wakings, early, from deep sleep or shallow,
That was the local blackbird, first solo
And after, to the chorus of a dozen doves;
As light becomes more largely evident,
Sparrows rap from the parapets,
And flitting in and out the gutter, chirrup.

Mariushka soon, her elfin smile, her silver trays,
Breakfast her scene, applause, bouquets, and kisses –
I must memorialise instanter somebody's arrival
From Charleston. Who? Encumbered
With wedding gifts, he tells me of his daughter
Shortly to wed the proprietor of Le Bombardier.

'My tibia anterior tends to ache.'
'My lungs – my captors;'
His calm, despite the foreign taxi-ride,
This chill in the air, sky with puffs
Of Raoul Dufy cumulus above us both,
Far as we are from Darfur, from Java,
From the Gaza Strip and what goes on
There and there. 'These days any squit
Can manufacture ruins in a wink.'

A clatter of wheels crossing cobblestones
When another traveller hauls
Past the oleander bush, beneath the sycamore
Stuffs to be apparelled in, embarked
On the trip of a lifetime –
Also askance this wallpaper I memorialise,
Outfits from the eighteenth century,
People prod a giant marrow bulging from the ground;
Lovers in a gondola slung under a Montgolfier balloon;
Near several prone sheep a man dangles a parasol.

Then, heard on a swerve, the repetitions:
Children singing loud and clear from school
A complicated anthem in their echoing
Assembly hall, arpeggios on the piano –
Elation, elasticity, a pattern models the air
As when, as when for pity's sake
Hölderlin felt it, took it for a beacon
Planted by some disconcerting gods
Tenuously under contract still,
Vague as the covenant became, to the likes of us.

Even so don't stop there though the hustle
Panics memory, bless me, how awkward now –
Tudela or Battuta, which to memorialise?

Wasn't it one of them commits to words of power
The singing of Constantinopolitan children;
A pervasive music stole upon him as he wandered in
The maze of monasteries crumbling thereabouts:
And what they sang of, did they precisely know?
That might have been two centuries, even,
Before the city, all its instruments betrayed,
Its ruins more conspicuous than ever,
Opened to the army of the Barbarian.

(*Paris, Hôtel des Grandes Ecoles*)

The Very Capable Waitress

Jacklyn's gesture
resting briefly her head
on the barman's breastbone
then, revived, effortless
raising it,
god knows, as might
a swan or a dolphin –
can it be time alone
soaks only to clarify
these timeless things.

Calligraphy

Aha, I find the late fourth century pope Damasus
Had seen to it that the tombs of martyrs

Were given fresh distinction by calligraphy.
With a calligraphy from his own pen old stones

Were incised by a mason selected not only
For his dexterity, also for his sympathies.

How different it is, that order of things,
From the reburial, pronto, of carving dismembered

By the constructors of emporia and office blocks
Over the sunken city in modern Mylasa –

What do the planners care about things Greek,
Ancient inscriptions or extended gods

Who still cling with touches of sunlight
To fluted stone scheduled for reburial?

If mind did not become a Mylasa, who'd recall
The crates of American rifles in summer 1940,

And how the girls and boys of freedom lift
Those greased guns from the crates in England,

Old grease, with rags wipe every vestige off,
Clots of grease hidden in the dark magazines?

Plain or grainy, the wooden rifle butt,
Polish it up until it glows

Fitting snug into your skinny shoulder –
An age before you knew what calligraphy was.

A Grackle with a Greek Motif

As if the wind had many borders,
The sharp angle it was open at –
Orange beak of the grackle-cock, the solo
Busily grooming boat-tailed grackle-cock –
Had many borders, many,

Much as Louise alleges, of the wind.

So too some laughter, in a twilit bar,
Of secretaries having a real blast –

As if to groom the grackle-cock was hoisting
First one wing to peck at, then the other:

All at once, from black and glossy
Plumage it has saturated, a cascade of lights
Rushes out, as if to meet the eye, welcome it,

Whooping and cartwheeling iridescence,
Momentary hues it would be hard to name –

Borders are spilled, others the eye eliminates.

Capacious they too could have been,
Those nothing-nits the beak was open for,

As if the uncontainable had been contained
In grackle-flesh, as if in feathers

The wind revolved its borders, let them go.

The Veil

… that surplus
which is the fragrance of things.
Roberto Calasso

It has to be the inconstant grizzling of the cicadas
The waste of time in ignorance of time
Fragility in the fading of that sound
The moment of hush begins with their whispering
Another when all together suddenly stop
And silently the wondrous gift is given

    Veil appears from veil
       State after state is generated

It has to be those long summer afternoons
Elsewhere the young loving bodies interlaced
Grizzling over them the cicada wave sound
Every now and then
      Remembered every now and then
(Who knew, late in the day you ask,
           Just what was going on)
Fading on the instant only to begin again
In memory with its trouble – in its painted cave
And out
The time irreversible
    Unrecoverable time.

From Rilke (March 1924)

Sap darkly renews itself in the roots
And comes to light again, and nourishes
Pure green so shy it still will be
Sheltering under woodbark from the winds.

The inner side of nature comes alive.
Still it is hushed, the new command Rejoice.
A whole year's youth is being lifted up,
Unrecognised as yet, in the stiff shrubs.

On the outside grey and cool, the laudable form
Of the old nut tree fills again with future;
Yet young foliage holds it in and shivers
When small birds perch, feeling it already.

The Holly Branch

The oldtime Flemish painters,
How well they did respect
Local objects, with qualities arcane,
As if they supposed,
As Proust came to suppose,
Reality itself to be mental.
Here for example is
Rogier van de Weyden at 42
Giving everything he's got
To a particle of creation,
He paints a torn-off
Branch of holly.
Rogier knew nothing of barbed wire
Yet made his holly just as spiky –
See, too, where this branch
Was torn perhaps accidentally
Loose, low down the white wound.
Every dancing leaf of the holly
Is darkened as it should be,
Or alight at innumerable
Angles or intersections,
Today in clouded weather,
Freeze everywhere, a pond
Perhaps in the vicinity

Vivid with people skating:
Yet these leaves are various too,
Shades of green, from dull to emerald,
So rushing through the uniform
Deep black background,
Could April now be far behind?
Here's the thing, even if,
Of course, it is doomed
Now to die: Just in time
Rogier takes care of it. Praise be
That no moral attaches to it,
For the painter made it
Happen with highlights
And spikes that make you
Shudder still.

Mole-Catching

1

Dividing earth and air
A mole lifts its tunnel's roof:
So I remember well the hope
Dashed early in the morning –
My steel trap's upper arms
Across the tunnel's track
Had not been sprung apart.

If they were spread,
The trap, its grippers
Underneath, athwart the track,
Had been released.
A mole might very well be in it.

I'd look into the mole's face then
And flick the snout. Still alive?
If so I'd try to crush the skull.
Enough, the pressure of two thumbs.
I skinned the moles. I cured (to make a hat)
Their velvet skins with alum and saltpetre.

A fat lot of use that was.
With moles the forest acres rippled.
Yet I was doing, perhaps, my bit.
No moles undermined the cricket pitch.

Since those days, turning often back,
I seem to have joined the party
Of moles. Not the clandestine kind.
More for circumspection than for sabotage.

So today, photographed by a friend,
I am not unconsoled by the result:
Eyes I could not open wider,
The jowls, the snout, the wary look,

The tuft of hair that could have been velvet,
Isn't the visage that of an animal trapped,
Blind enough to imagine, unembittered, an escape?

Between this earth and air, almost seven
Decades later, those not so nimble moles
Did stage some sort of a comeback.

2

As for the thriving of moles
I never did give it a thought.
Not once did I wonder how,
Or what with, moles did it.
Not once was a couple at it
Revealed, or the result:

A wiggly velvet infant.

A limp dead mole in my fist –
And now, for symmetry, at last
A balance can be redressed:
A metaphysical vacuum I could fill
With fantasies I'm loth to depict.
Belly to belly? Belly to back?
Did she admit his marly prick
With all four shovels digging in?

3

The small black beast scratching a tunnel out –
From the fit of this costume I should not step.
Or else I plug with fables, celestial intrigues,
Metaphor, buzzword, the icy gap through which
Deep space by chance pumps influential winds,
And heaves (as I scratch) unfathomable sighs.

Figures of speech can have fatal consequences.
Also the trapped mole is no stranger to symmetry.
Devil-knows-what prompting my thought to fly
I fall off the face of the earth. So I suppose
A telling need to invoke does propel the organism.
Should I hereafter invoke no real matter at all,
Not catch fire from divinity nailed to a cross?

Surely the vengeance of moles will provide
For a tunnelling on and on. Though tunnels
I quit collapse behind me, they do collapse
Back into earth and air. Line by line I arrive
In air for the amiable who live to let live;
Significant air, for that we go tunnelling, moles.

Lyric of the Dove

From what ark escaped
Where too much croaking was
Flew possibly a dove.

A perfect dove, so crossing
A field of steel and tarmac
She was their cancellation.

A line dead straight.
Through living air she flew,
Wings, only twice they beat,

Then spread, slow for a dip,
Again for a sudden uplift
Shut, she disappears

Into an actual tree,
Alone at last, unfelt
The limb her talons grip.

Goonhilly Downs (1939)

No tilted stones, menhir or cromlech,
Only for what seemed miles around
Mauve, or white, the tiny
Heather flowers, their cups I thought
Formal as crinolines.
There, crisscrossed by paths
Hardly broader than rabbit runs,
The flat land took me in;
At several intersections of the paths,
Or no, just one or two, little heaps
Of flint had been deposited. Not one
Implement did I discover,

Walking fresh from the sea,
And how on earth had I got there?
There, to be touched,
As by a spirit, touched – who heard

The gull cry in the old time here? Or
If this ground housed the plover,
If, spent into me, the Norfolk plover's
Forked mew had been copying time,
The come and go, here and now I'd make
A human hinge between two wings.

Such high drama could not undo
The spell of heather, in leftover flint
Something imminent, a puzzle in the breeze,
For I was unread, not here at home,
But eerily a presence was irradiating
Me, at every step almost
Catching my breath, and thrilled,
Knowing that this must be.

Today I only meant to point
At the place. Its much older name
Most maps reject. Soon that boy shook
His delusion off. Old men
Become so ordinary, rambling on.

Hammersmith

Now on each side emptily the traffic
Woffles and guffaws, in her purple apron
Bobbie K stoops to identify –
Suited to the supper table – a good flower.
Bell, the while, busy lissom cat,
All snow and jet and marigold,
Hunches alert among some infant ferns.

She's listening for a frog, frog like fern
A green to pounce upon, to capture.
Infant ferns constitute for Bobbie
Possibly a kind of vegetable fabric:
Weaving is her art, up and down the land
Throats and shoulders carry her glowing scarves.
One fragile moment gathered whole shows how
Community in cat and weaver prospers.
This here archaic whisper starts in solitude –
Welcomed or cold-shouldered by the crowd
The poem that became of it returns thereto.

Memorabilia of February 9, 2008

Small, I wake, in a cot, and there she stands, benign, in black
and white, with a headband, stooping she sets on the foot of
the cot, full of good things, a high-handled basket, which in
the morning, when I sit up to see, is not there.

A hut built from junk, not far from the tulips I'd torn to
pieces, wondering at the stamens. Before hiding there, I'd felt
so good underneath the grand piano.

Scattered screech of pheasant before thunderstorm at Old
Buckenham Hall, woodland all around. Soft fur of young
rabbit I'd caught by hand and killed.

In perhaps 1946 an old woman's fingers hold the handle of a
magnifying glass, she sits at a low window scrutinising faded
script on a yellowed sheet of paper; her window looks out on
that short flagstoned alley not far from Addenbrooke's, not
quite opposite the Fitzwilliam.

Of Bernard Spencer on the couch in Mahmoud's flat, the
crossed knees (Oxford, late Spring 1952).

As my father ran from the Schaffhausen ferry for the bus to Zürich, his silver hair fluttering, my fear for him.

Mary barefoot under the rose trellis; her face, beautiful features undistorted, while she came at me with the carving knife.

In Langtry there was a hut with an old Indian woman in it, mummified.

In our toilet a millipede at least nine inches long, its claws like sickles, or the kris in those stories for boys. And curling unnoticed under the boot of the utility man, the coral snake's tail.

Hypatia at 60 being dragged out of her chariot, stripped, killed and flayed by Christian converts in an early church. (Alexandria).

Two girl neighbours, one trailing the other, talking as they cross the parking lot, observed by me, at my dusty desk, deciding I'll remember in future the names Eratosthenes and Ctesibius.

Among rocks on the slope up to the little orchard at River Hills, its brilliant blue eyes, prehistoric angularity, stillness, dignity, the alligator lizard. As if it had dropped there out of another but still current time, as if it was studying for the first time an utterly alien being.

Samuel Palmer's Ghost Goes Scavenging

Heroes, animals, utensils
    Flew up into the night sky,
Stuck to stars. They never yet
    Fell down flat; flatten, though,
They did, the constellations ...
    Traherne, so ravish'd, for a fortnight
He could scarsly Think or speak
    Of anything else, discovered, infinit,
Points of space, while heavens opened
    More and more into his comprehension,
Limit giving way to limit, everlasting
    Magnitudes the soul so intimately knew
They are enjoy'd like Things in a cabinet ...
    I will not go to the dead dolphin
Or sniff through seaweed for a sodden cap
    (Once there was a boot, the foot was in it).
I'll track instead over sand flatts
    Shallow puddles, into pools by the tide
Squandered across a spit of rock I'll peer.
    In my graphite pocket, should I find them,
Cowrie shells, grooved and ribbed, a pyramid
    Or tiny cube of serpentine, glass
Shards, the green all but
    Whisked out of them, by futile motion
Substances rubbed opaque,
    May not unwelcome sit. Of Strand brats hopping
Before his window, I heard the old man volunteer:
    Heaven designs their voices. I contract
Into these portable forms Fountain Court
    Remembered, Shoreham subjective too;
Or else, done wrong for its own skin, inflated
    A bubble freedom bursts. Yet then
A Fig, another time he tutted,
    A Fig for the Corporeal ...

A Symbolist

What if it all had been foretold,
all his moves and imaginings,
by the book that travels
glistening every single night
in the flow of stars,
all but the moment
the road, his road of air and water,
rose up and struck him
dead, so fortunately
milking out of poetry the venom pettiness,
he let the time it kept disappear into the Everything.

Goldfinches

> *The expiatory power of violence*
> *is not visible to men.*
> Walter Benjamin

A mind awakening, how does it hop
Unprompted, in no time at all,
Shut-eyed still, from a flash
Of yellow and green to the shorn
Top of a hedge, manicured, privet?

From sublimated deposits
(Their combination known to sleep)
The home-cured formulae erupt –
Percepts, pictures, equations marvellous
And sometimes algebraic.

Unprompted, in no time at all,
Surely not so. And think again, the question
How could be a blind:
Evade, it must, overlay a harder one
It fatefully suppressed.

Why, why not a fusion
Into the prodigy? A harmless
Blink and reality quickens. The hedge,
Out of it flock the goldfinches cocooning
Every last Inquisitor's head.

So manifold on human backs
Is responsibility heaped, hear now
For relief that in moist, shady places
From fern fronds drop spores that turn
Into the tiny individual go-between gametophytes,
And those, once fertilised, bring ferndom on.

The Inventor

Heron of Alexandria, city of The Mind,
                              has perched
In a semi-precious metal tree
Two mechanical birds that sing,
And in a tree right there beside
                    squats an owl who turns
And glares at the birds with such a rancour
They stop their singing, terrified.

The Victorian Photo

(For the painter Malcolm Bucknall
who copied and modified it)

Linked flank to flank like bacteria
                under the microscope
Such pretty ones. Watchful her expression
The dark girl with a long face
On his right. See what an abundance of lace
Falls in a triangle across her breast.

                      Doubtless,
On his left, the mother. Her face now pudgy,
Shocked she looks askance as if she heard
Their doorbell ringing. In his right hand
Her own has settled, but his left crept
Across her spine to dangle now
                from her left shoulder.

                   Cringing,
Elbow pressed on mother's thigh, does this boy
Not look to you for help? He's out of sorts,
He's fretful, heavens, is not mother's other hand
Nestled in his crotch? No, and how indecent
The very thought of it. Meanwhile
The gentleman wears with a flourish,

                Sharp in profile against
An indistinct laurel hedge the gardener's boy
Clipped to rhyme with their imaginings
Of classical Greece, the head, snout up, ears
Big and pointed,
Of a most cheerful porker. Here he is:
Lord Acorn, who discovered
How liberalism too can turn a profit.

Laugh yourself silly then, shuddering at this
Nightmare of a regression
So domestic that nobody notices.

Daubigny's Mill

From sky the colour of pee
Did it hang so heavily, after all,
The huddle of these huts?

Mud sustains. The shining oblong
Streams. Bare trees branch up capturing
To variegate the hill slope.

The oblong glassy, beside it,
Waking now or for sleep
Assembled, a flock of ducks,

Each duck tiny, included
And particular; but was it raw,
This twilight, not warmed by memory?

A little window pierces brown.
Newly splashing, whitewash,
Here this wall, that wall –

Rhetoric elsewhere rules the roost,
Gallery walls house the classic
Sporty gods, bread-gobbling heroes.

Oh no, slime is not the heart of this,
Credit such somber harmonies
(Day darkens or a day begins), they

Help a woman freshen her lips,
Man take a future to mind. Why,
The night it died, baby screams –

What a stink here, even so:
Outhouse, pig dung. A tinted picture,
His breath of incense, our Redeemer –

And home is home. A cat
Presides on a shoulder. Old dog
Welcomes a pat on the head:

The want, here again, feeling it
A cupped hand kindly frigs
Dewlap fur, mastoid, breastbone.

In a Hammock between Trees

A rare high wind blew last night,
A rare wind and high like time
Made a roaring in tall oaks,
Set the juniper shuddering
And blew, like time, all sorts of stuff around.

The old settlers knew also of the wind,
Suffering from its rages often, just as now
Where the tornado rips through,
Horrible twisting tunnels
Mangle the bodies, roll them flat.

Even the ants know, at work, the wind
And its building in time
Tiny new shapes in their dust, ant-pinnacles,
Ant-ravines, ant-piazzas
Rise up out of nowhere at a gesture
Of the wind, or so they saw, the old settlers.

Doubtless they invented therefore
A pure self, intangible, yet
Figuratively in touch with timeless being.

Such projective purity imagined upon that self
Had a man be god with it.

If only to be *with* anything at all
Did not obscure, did not violate this purity,
It followed that every tiny span
Of years was a note or two in the symphony
Of everything. So it was arguable that the world,
Minus accidents, should be
Essentially music.
                    Enchanting figment:
Pure self as a dancer
To cosmic permutations –
The progression, inexorable, and repetitions,
Also the variations of a music, spirited changes –
How chromatic the figment
Of timeless possibility discharging itself
In chords that thrilled through matter
Melodies lifting, harmonies carrying
Embodied souls along, wrapped as they might be
In their whirlwinds. Birds,

Birds could flit and hop in the spirals,
For five thousand years one song theirs to sing –
On occasion purposefully.

                         In between,
Agonies, also thoughts that slid
In and out of a consciousness, theirs,
The old settlers. *It*
Does not cohere. Friends of mine
Cannot dovetail for me even these shallowest
Contradictions. Even two measures
Of The Noon Witch infiltrate in vain
These cauldrons of noise,
                         the base brew of idioms
Where shouting happens. Adverse atmospheres
Remind me still of timelessness
As a theme, as an absence merely. How
And to whom now should I convey this gist:
That what was not was worth having lived for?

From Doctor Clown

Elsewhere, from its husk,
That night you found me
Too frightening to love, faultless,
Weary no more, done with
Inching up and up
From underground, a briefly
Golden cicada flew.

At 80

High overhead four motors drone
While dishes clink in Sarah's kitchen.
Next our blackbird with a titter
Stops one song to figure out another.
High time I heard a spirit speak,
But am amazed in Paris how the swallows
Rake this rotunda of the skies
For joy and small diverting flies.

Of the Belovèd Someone

Confused about that which
Touches nothing, without which
There would have been nothing,

Attend to it a moment,
Attend: as it retrieves,
On this day like no other,

A joy, once to have felt in it
Nothing to be acknowledged,
From an impact uplift, at the utmost

A breath, when close, a touch
Of the belovèd someone –
Immediately wide-awake to it

Now, perceiving it diffused
Among new leaves, old spines
Of books perhaps, the moment

There is here again, the time
All felt afresh, not to be redeemed,
For so, only so, in this hive

Where entombed it wanders, this body,
Not a word for it can ego there pin down,
Rare the trope, moonlit vapour of

Syntax or instrument agile, agile
Enough to contain its tremor, still
Opening Memory first

It begins Forever, even, briefly,
When, with a light, a distant laughter,
The Door has closed.

Savanna Rose

Just what would she know of it,
Of this antique turbulence –

Merest slip of a girl
But history shook up.

Time and again you scoot
In and out of mine –

No idea how short
Mine now likely is,

Yours a restriction long
With hope deferred.

Then, sugarpie forever
Lost in advance,

Never remote like Beatrice,
Soon you saw through my ego trip

Me wanting only to fish
For fresh heart in your torrent,

Where constellations glow afloat
Yet extravagance is forgone.

Some Birds

I swallowed that third benedictine probably
too soon, but as to birds,
      the barn owl on his beam,
kestrel swivelling on a shaft of air
                  and the seagull with a squawk,
and no perceptible effort gliding –
there is beauty in birds and all about them,
the ways their plumage
      fits the planes
            or tunnels in the air,
a wholeness to their colours –

how about that? And their varieties
from any sparrow scuffling in his dust
to cobalt blue legs, the white silken breast
and metallic green spot above the eye
      of the kingbird described by Wallace,
from the friendly redbreast poised
on the handle of a spade that somebody

left dug into the soil of a drab garden,
to the condor in the Andes with a wingspan
   four times as far as anyone can reach.

No Roman prelates here to aim at them
      their shotguns, no Calabrians
to cut down all the trees …

Birds appear also in plays such as that
   of Aristophanes.
Tio tio tinx the Greek actor calls replicating
sounds I heard while performing in English
the play out of doors
on a ranch in Texas: spluttering Greek
we strode on a slope and an actual bird
mocked from a bush by the creek
tio tio tinx (though a time-warp
crept in here somehow). The thousand songs
that rush from the birds when Spring
is what they feel – what life
what future might there be on earth without birdsong
   to brace, to console, to welcome us.

The swan solicitous beside her cygnet,
      survivor of five, the others
         gobbled by raccoons – or snapping turtles –
Could I ever, believing birds, have even
gone halfway only with Paul Celan? Since when
         did a new coherence between
ourselves and undivided nature
cease to be thinkable?

Hummingbird, how should we greet your
         individual occurrence, let alone the scores
of astonishingly robust varieties? Thrush,
missel thrush plucking his worm
      from a lawn in Rutland,
Aztec parrot flitting from a palm
among creekside huts in Michoacan,

that erratic wren who flew
round my desk one day and out again –
what sort of world flashed into its perception?

    No self-denial there, turning bitter into life-denial,
monkish wheel and rack ...

What position, however, do their tribes
and habits occupy in the global food-chain?
    A large one now as it must always have been,
    depending on
vagaries of space-time. Come to think of it,

earthbound I glimpse through vertigo
    gradual and huge mutations. Alas,
lonesome the loon calls back birds of Ur,
birds of Babylon,
for brilliant breeds have perished probably,
what spectacular doves, what secret songs,
what willingness to be, to be ...

And unforgotten, nested once in fathomless night,
a million golden birds,
an enormous whisper of lifted wings
now you flock, vigour to be
in time to come,
in the exile of daylight

Tiberius must have seen the swifts off Isca

    skim the calm and turquoise water
and heard their quick shrill cries
    while tumultuous round rocky nests they flutter;
and horses in whose fat were carried
spores of the very first fragrant flowers
        heard as anyone today can do
various birds, calling perfectly.

Among Events Unreported

Year after year uncoiling,
Coiling again strung out along
A telephone cable,
Wistaria vines multiply blossom,
Perspire fragrance,
But for the bees, to no end whatever.
Upward whiteness gushes,
Down it cascades, like
Rapids arrested: no, more precisely wild
Palomino ponytails.
From tendrils, how perilous,
The long lanciform
Beanpods dangle, and
When a herd in file passes overhead
Shake, till air at a distance
Dissolves its prodigies —
The drumming of hundreds of hoofs.

The Boy and the Piano

Upstairs in his bed
He heard the wheels of trains
Click over jointed rails,
The coal rush down a shaft
Into the tender; he could smell
Coal in the air, only coal

                    ★

While down below
Father's fingers on the keyboard
Frighteningly brushed
Across his hearing
And felt for his darkest hollows
As fingers cross a drumskin.

⋆

How should he now recall
From his ancient books
A secret constellation of the inner life?
Remains, for a will of their own,
A flowing of the hollows into one –

⋆

Neither loves nor projectiles,
Nor atmospheric alteration yet
Reached into it, the dot,
Surely for something else
The target.

Some Remaining Masonry

1

The Balconies

For Helena de la Fontaine

Always in Paris it is Spring.
In such pure daylight
lustrous cafés line
every little street
and men wear
at jaunty angles their berets,
baked a crisp and golden brown
the baguette
tucked underneath an arm, as everybody knows,
they come dancing up now and then
as if to kiss
the lifted hands

of girls who lean
and smile
from balconies bejewelled with flowers.

2

The Column

He knows he should be doing
Something significant here.
Something even memorable.
In Paris, it is the month of May
When riots did happen, flowers

Do bloom, and this is the year
Of deep cleavage, breasts nearly tangible.
But he just strolls about, or sits
Listening to the shouts, or to the singing
Of schoolgirls, to footsteps

That knock across the paved garden.
Early there the magpie grates its teeth.
There, supposing death will not forget her,
He'll turn his eyes, what's left of them,
On the roughly reassembled column,
Five cubes of Merovingian limestone.

An Apparition

When the groan of traffic
        Is diminished to a mumble,
All three windows open now,
        And penetrating night you hear
From one of those huge-antlered
        Local Spanish oaks a dove
Quietly coo – Lucretius

Is confirmed: *Thy influences*
Pierce first the bird-heart.

Not motionless, a very distant shining
    Will widen soon its acute angle
(Constantly around the mass burst
    Unimaginable lightnings);
Then to become its hypotenuse
    How shall our perch not tremble,
Old sages not trace in dust
    Momentary dances,
Sweep through our time
    Those vistas bending,
And reason, restive not by chance,
    Desperately take wing.

Poem Forty-Four

The fresh-leafed woodland,
    a cuckoo calling in it;
Tapering shins
    of girls who grow up poor –

Even if it is he alone who disappears,
From all he loved he is being taken.

Hottish and quite wet the air,
    Spring time, night, but the bird
Wakes with tuneless short shrieks
    to scarlet replication nature,

Mocking but with no mockery – spry again
    I also from a bartop memo

Copy: He is being taken
    away from all he ever loved.

How can the herebelow go as deep
    as in time you feel it must have been –

Those fine young people over there,
    what more are they willing to do?

The Old French Wine Glass

Who's now to know how it was made:
A glass-blower standing there mid vats
That seethe with liquid to be scooped;
Pressed to his lips, his cheeks
Rosy, bursting with spare air,
Something like a post-horn,
And all in one single puff expelled?
Shell and stem and base?

Halfway up one strip of the shell
A tiny bubble baffles the physicist:
Remnant of what the glass-blower
Blew through his horn into space,
To tweak and have encircling air fashion it –

Deep in the inverted dome of which
Now some red wine waits;

To ponder its attraction in this
Amalgam of the four elements
Exactly like a star
The bubble disdains. Exactly
Like the question as to love
Flung back in a lover's face.

Homage to Alkan

Probably, led by a little girl,
I'm walking out, in 1865 or so, my white stick
Tapping among the roses for the right path
Which even she is not altogether
Certain of. No, probably it is twenty ten,
Late Spring, our village is in France,
Burgundy precisely, not far off somebody
Strums on the piano happily in tune
A composition by Alkan, an old one too,
His *Petit conte* with its quite mischievous
Grace-notes and trills in high registers.
Probably, as on we plod, I'm first of all
Troubled by a thought – old X, his novelettes
And ravings, don't they achieve magnitudes
My own endeavours lacked? Some of them
Bloom, over and again (mine are not annual).
But does it matter now? Probably
Not. At eighty-four you put up with everything
Except these impersonations of God,
Besides, they haven't started the war yet
And this village blackbird now
Starts to quote notes from Alkan's *Conte*
Among the village chimney pots. Probably,
Too, the air in Burgundy is arranging
To house a marvel of a harvest, already
You can catch a whiff of it in fresh air
That's, well, how to put it, ripe,
At least with fragrance ripening. So on we plod
And the little girl is probably
A grand-daughter, misty little thing
I can barely see, though her touch
Thrills me through. Not chattering now
She is leading me past the graveyard.
Probably none of my relatives there
Would complain if I were to substitute
For their names, momentarily, I mean
In thought, in rose-petal probability,

The names of some uncanny composers
Whose influences chastened my lines. Yes,
Probably, inside the little church,
Where faint incense is spliced with mould,
Great black tombstones let into the floor
Carry names and dates that ask for wonder,
Cut by crafty chisels (so you can hear
The mason wheeze, the mallet tap)
Calligraphically into them. No,
What is it, the real thing? Probably
I could have pursued the reverie
With the sight of a four-masted clipper
Cleaving the mist, though here is Burgundy;
It is sailing in later than was expected,
Cargo however intact, probably careening
Superbly with a salt west wind astern,
For, Alkan, there it does come in,
You hear the gulls hungrily yelping,
The splash of porpoises caracolling,
And that old ship creaking throatily,
Was this the thing? Probably it was not.
What's to be done with an old ship or for it?
But let it float, probably, so
That expression may be bright and early,
That vigour for the new may sustain
In souls a passion for the immaterial,
That the straws of Burgundy be brought in dry.

The Pepper Brandy

And what of their ability to build
The Greek clock into a Tower of Winds?

What of the wires attached to the naked
Arab they had hooded with a cloak?

Was the operating procedure standard?
What court should decide? And was it

Conspicuous waste forced a feeble Ptolemy
To pawn great Alexander's golden coffin?

Ah, but the spheres – it has been said
They drive, like a wast shadow, time –

Whereat complacently a Golushkin
Gulps his glass of pepper brandy down.

The Enjoyment of Shouting

Any road, averse to shouting
And the enjoyment of shouting,
If ever I did raise my voice
I had first to steady my voice.

Could no form of words quell the brutality rising …

The empty armour shakes as the cygnet moves:
But bar the shouting, in flood Scamander,
Was it all over? For the boys, in bronze armour,
Those names, all over bar the shouting?

Vestigios de España

... None of them doctored soda pads
    ever did scour our pannikins.
Water was all, if there was any.

Mouldy bread stank finer than urine.
    Why now ladybird scuttle on past,
If out on elbow I make to lean?

All is water. Tasted of tin it did,
    bean stew faintly steaming.
Never enough of that

In our pannikins. Equals, us. Not all
    the bullets flew overhead. Not often
Came time for some good fucking ...

Otherwise than with a professional army
    you'll not beat the shit out of Fascists.
Not so long before we stood up and shouted

There were pianos playing Goyescas;
    the sweet notes float from rooms in provinces;
in the Duero country, people sullen and stunted;

Don Antonio reciting with children the alphabet.

The Vine that Lost its Elm

What is it hurries me so
No holes can be located
In water? No roofs
Of thatch on the steppe, so long
As I eat my heart out?

Slip somehow I have to,
A ravine grumbles,
With force the transitive
Persistent flux propels all;
Rosemary, the bread dipped in oil,
Hold fast no more.

You it was, day or night,
Could straighten me,
Still me. Remember we saw
Once, once we saw woodsmoke
Spiral up the chimney,

White doves flutter,
A farmstead in the ravine,
Ravine become an orchard, even.

Today

Le beau jour vient, de lueur revêtu
Quand Phébus ha son cerne fait …
                                    Louise Labé

Today is when the thought occurs that time visits earth
disguised as a colossal world-enveloping tube, its envelope
being of no alien substance but the tube's own persistently
ongoing churning contents.

   Now I perceive that the tube sucks as well as blowing out;
that history leapfrogs from condensation to vaporisation, as
does a *moi* for Baudelaire, for Louise Labé three hundred years
before him.

   Down the tube everything goes. Shrinking in the volatile
perspective of mortals, us vigilant but unskilled workers after
all, the tube narrows at the far end proportionately as we
surface and congregate; so the tube expanding came to be
pictured as a tapering cornucopia.

Today, too, how suddenly, with an earthquake, fragrance of a musk rose fathomless, penetrating the tangled twitter of a dawn chorus the fluted call of an oriole, summer comes in again. Strolling through long egg-yellow and leafgreen grass the lady in white appears; she wears on a tilt a dainty sunhat, holds on a tilt an emerald parasol. Still the galaxy is humming, so we are informed, humming a faint echo of the big bang, a humming you might detect with instruments at night on an alp; maybe then on the bang you'd choose to bestow an apter name, Epiphany of Chance.

Hearing Martha Argerich perform *Gaspard de la Nuit*, her steel spring fingers at the keyboard like white birds flocking, I enjoy, but with terror, as through an acoustic keyhole, a spectacle of the essence and qualities and measureless variety of time present as it should have been, pouring into the open from the hands of the unknown. For now there is only this proliferation of particulars, irreducible to the One, and the Plenum recognises itself, if at all, in the perfect and instantaneous defiance of a music turning, as abstrusely as the motes that associate in a shaft of sunlight, to attack the blur, the stagnation, the beast within. From its deep bed in time you heard it surge, the outcry after the hush of sacrifice. Might all be well now? Can this only be Ravel?

The Laundress

Bothering us for a long time,
This laundry woman: Beneath
A blue segment of sky she is
All brown and profiled against
A cliff so laboriously hewn
That it resembles a rampart.
Like a baby mask her face,
Black crescent moons for eyebrows
And greys to streak her bodice,
But yellow or brown the rampart
Towers behind the woman, as if

Its gravity propelled her – darkly
Her combed hair clings to the head
She launches forward, stooping.
Awkward skirts impede her,
Surely now she has to be hurrying
Somewhere. A little daughter
Runs at her left side, one foot
Lifting off the shadowy ground,
Hurled stooping forward she
Mimics her mother, and the labour
Extracted from the mother, that
She will inherit too. Still,
Goya's glimpse of them has put
Happy family bonding into question:
Are they running to the fountain
Or to the river at all? Are they
Running away from something
Hidden? Their velocity
Must have to do with bread. Yet
Won't they have had to scoot,
In those times, across the picture,
Basket on the mother's haunch
Bumping up and down on it, because
Shirts coiled in the wickerwork
(Where bristles dashed, dripping
White, the profile of a billygoat)
Had been stiff with blood, or wet?
The next up for execution
Needed snowy linen, so the French
Bullets could be met with decent
Spanish gestures, death be dignified,
You now conjecture, whereupon
Some villagers in bleached
Apparel sign to us how best not
To die, if only, in Bordeaux,
Goya, to assuage despair, stands
Candle-crowned for half the night,
Imagining, him, in grief and detail,
Horrors he had likely never seen.

Symposium

Listen, when they speak,
Beyond help,
Some spiritual,
Some tormented,
Of what will not be spoken.
Listen, even underneath
Party hats, behind
The novelty nose, the shower
Of empty bottles flung.

★

Hardest die the worst old habits.
To manage wars, to squeeze
Money from his presses, tubes
And dismembered bodies,
A Murdoch will be wangling:
Show me an age innocent of atavism,
Untrampled by the mastodon, communities
Feeling, but with caution, for their dead.

★

In a sort of people, powers
Have to be confined;
If they break out, evil,
Run for it, recoup, resist
Too late, and given half a chance
They slithered into us.

Trampoline

Why did they picture for us Dionysus' dong
So charmingly? Sublime
The tree in flower, never to be gnarled.

The cords that sprang to help prolong
Your decorative life in time,
They became tortuous, slack, and snarled.

Now halfway blind, not quite yet bald,
Drive a fist deep down through the grime,
Bring up a new song.

Pavane

In that green girl was death or madness.
Mad she became, from time to time.
As to death I have no information.
Yet our dead make of mind a magnifying glass
As long as now the thought of her can change
To tracks of fire burnt across a green
The shadow of the branching of these trees.

From Georg Trakl

... *Merciful God, let me hope once again.*
                                    S. Kierkegaard, *Journal* (1841)

Reverie

Hedges fill with fragrances,
And between them couples walk, in love;
From the road, now dusk is falling,
Cheerful customers arrive.

In the tavern yard, pensive, a chestnut tree;
The moist bells are not chiming any more;
Beside the river, a boy singing –
Fire, in search of something dark –

O blue stillness! O patience!
When all is busily flowering –

Night, do give the homeless person
Peace of mind,
Darkness unfathomable,
A golden moment in the wine.

Psalm II

So quiet, this autumn,
As if, swivelling heads, prone at the foot of a wall,
Blind men listened for the ravens' flight;
Across father's face the sunlight flickering;
Old the village, perishing amid peaceable oaks;
Red forge, hammer blows a heartbeat;
Hush, for among the jostling sunflower heads
In slow hands the housemaid buries her face,

Rooms fill with silence and with fear;
Old women walk with slow steps;

A crimson mouth dissolves into the dark.
Evening with wine, taciturn. A moth, nymph
In a shroud of bluish sleep, dropped from the beam,
Farmboy slaughters lamb in yard, we are dazed
By the sweet smell of blood; cool dark well-shaft;
Asters droop, golden voices in the wind,
You look at me at night with eyes all mould,
I watch your cheeks rot into immobile blue.

A weed bonfire, soon quenched, the black tarn speaks no more;
As if from its Calvary Hill the Cross came striding down,
And without one word earth expelled her dead.

Inscription in an Old Album

Always, melancholy, you come back again,
The lonesome soul surrenders;
In a golden glow let day conclude.

Patience, now the pains flow in; brim
With harmony, be humble, a little bit unhinged,
Look! – a touch of twilight.

Night comes again, a mortal grieves;
Someone else is there to grieve with him.

Years pass, lower and lower
You will bow your head,
Shuddering under autumn stars.

In Slow Motion

For his own good reason hereabouts
A random owl
Observes between his hoots a silence.
Are his reflections empty then?
What might he suppose
Of mouse or toad, of cockroach even,
Abstractly relishing
Foods in his solitary silence,
Might they ask? On its own branch of time
Each animal must sit. Ah, Mrs Sewell,
So prim she would not put a name
To the furball of an owl-turd I'd found.

The next hoot has yet to come.
So you chance to consider snow,
Beautiful and deadly snow
On high passes in the Caucasus,
Snow with flakes geometrically various
Caked Byzantine bricks that Iliazd saw,
Snow on those bricks in 1919
(In '45 great snows were to cake
The burned bricks heaped in Hamburg),
Also by Iliazd observed,
Snow on the moustache of a gypsy,
For gypsies risked survival
In pits and huts where once
Those selfsame bricks
Walled the Byzantine palaces.

A longer hoot. Again you glide
Over old letters of Iliazd the emigrant,
Recall the banknotes for exchange or sale in Pera,
Banknotes of a dozen brief republics
Already beaten down by the Bolsheviks;
And so feebly a cry
Crept into the skein of random reminiscence.

Banknotes and the snow,
Constantinople starlit, for the owls,
And less distress, more but slow drama
Circles the void an owl announces now,
Inscribed across whose hearing spin
Glyphs for the noises in his neighbourhood,
For every single sound that circles him
Marooned, should that be what they say,
Among these scrapings of the Word Unspoken.

Phantom Caravan

If I take two paces
      into the room
Not altogether
      harmlessly tonight
This dull red
      fossil of a bivalve,
From Mexico
      reportedly,
Now poised
      on a yellow file folder,
A heap of typescript
      underneath it,
Will spread a wing
      of shadow in the crosslight,
Open the Door
      to which I found no Key,
And be for a wink, vesperal, burning,
      a butterfly.

Byzantium Revisited

1

Return to Constantinople

Once the music of mating is hushed
And all the randy dancing done,
Passing by, won't she have waved to me,
The dowager empress, from the prow
Of her skimming mahogany steamboat,
With an invitation to breakfast?

2

Light and heavy: Daydreaming in Balat

Whereas for dinner time
A flinty emperor then prescribes
Ritual dancing by his Domestics ...

★

Traffic packed creeps hurtles hearing
Over anchovies crisp on a rooftop terrace
A seagull flip open its blank book
You might surmise that facing Marmara
A still continuous stone boundary wall
Quite weightily prefigured
Theunbrokenceremonialdroneofturkishspeech.

★

Streets tortuously entangle, steep or flat,
Dungbeetle city, still rolling its ball of dark times;
A piled tissue of gravity blots their value
Out of the noises, out of the misery;
For the old unseen techniques, go search
A waterfront, a holy image; the dogs

Howl at night because dogs always did so;
  Where Allah's breath
Blisters visible ground
People stream from pods of grey cement.

★

Deep inside the stone, it was said,
Roses hide; that sliced thin
The marble blooms,
So liquid 'it outshines any flower' –

★

You might glimpse as figures
In the depths of time
Patterns that rotate.

★

For it was an old garden, twilit,
And Eylem told how she left her body
But in horror at her sensation of the infinite
('Free, too free, pollen,
  No more free than pollen on the wind')
Got back in again quick. –

★

And did in ancient time those Greek poor
Also copulate in a labyrinth of ruins,
Was there no *there* for an exile to return to,
Did an emperor sip his posset from a dish of clay ...

3

Escape from Istanbul

Resist the urge
  to jump, Resist.
    Festoon the bridge

With fairy lights,
  turquoise to violet
    violet to emerald

Turning. Make sure
  the full moon
    over Asia rising

Beats her gong.
  As traffic thins,
    one quadrant more,

Then breathless travel
  beyond the houses
    to no end.

Another Melancholy

Stricken tree on a blasted heath, but also like a boy waving his
arms, bending his spine, and stamping his feet as he pounces
out of a hideyhole to scare the wits out of you, this domestic
angel is dancing.

  Each limb is a malformity, twisting, bloated, and from the
gnarled chunk of one leg a six-fingered fright of a hand
sprouts; wooden extruded tendons that break out from a tibia,
those also spawn, also sprouting from the chunk, a horned
demon antelope cavorting vertically up.

  Has a dead tree become such a bugaboo that it had to have
a vulture's head? Or could this be the head of the Bald Eagle,

grounded? The tibia collapses into a booted foot, shod as for swamp or desert warfare.

The other leg, or root, wears a distended medieval boot, unless it is, with a blue wrap flapping up to the knee, a bedroom slipper. Somehow this misbegotten Laokoön has swallowed its serpent.

The head tilts down, open-beaked, with a pointy tongue visible, and three teeth along the gum. The eye-socket is a yellow valve with a groove in it, grey-white the head, a striped muffler neck – and yet has the angel, dancing so, anywhere a body? No body, a bad spirit, who dances too.

The maker of this image had a thought: Home is where the chasm of the flesh opens. Where Michelangelo fought his unfinished battle; where the occupant wallows in it; where its smell and volume and texture crowd out everything. The faintest harmony in sex, the exhilaration of soul – eliminated. Gut-wrenched by that thought, the artificer gave the angel only enough body to hang some bedclothes and dish-cloths from.

Even then, for all its apparel, the stricken gesticulating tree whose vulture merged into the woodwork, to become a squawking Bald Eagle, has no body to admire.

That holds, even if one foot is at the moment stamping the ground.

For ground there is, a level green, nothing but green, though on the very low horizon may be detected, so very far away and yet right beneath a crotch-clout, a shining city on a hill. For the pink clout that flaps at the angel's crotch does resemble that article worn by some men aforetimes; with it they could clean the ooze from their infections.

The angel means to frighten you away. Or else it is screaming at you an invitation to dare approach the city. The sky is clouded. One streak of blue parallels the curve of the angel's rippled neck. To be guarding the city it is too close to you. It is dancing too far from that place, driven forwards by unappeasable spite, ever perhaps to have felt the very springs of desire, even after they have become a flood, release into the memory a taste of time that was to have come.

Slight Poems

Prologue
Ask Herodotus

Shall nobody ever know,
As the conflagration of flesh barrels along,
How the killers, flunky or king, the unfit
Makers of war with no end
But a bloating of corruption
And the torturer healthily willing to hack
Ears and noses off, the tongue, the breasts,
Stopped at the Gardens of Midas
Where, wild, and in all the world
The sweetest smelling
Sixty-petalled roses grow.

Aquatint

How he hankered after
The silence.
   Rose flowering, no,
Another day, rose
   Actually opening.
     Nakedness

Apparent when she will have
Stripped.
   In its husk of silence,
     a knee beginning

To press on the bed.
    Careful,
Howl for a holy moment,
    Not for the deserted street,
    Not for the sound of nothing.

An Exercise in Direct Discourse

On slaves who drank in Brazil
They clamped a mask of tin:

Holes for the eyes and nose, but not
For the mouth where drink got in.

You could take your slave to the smith
For a fitting. His doorposts by day

Were festooned with masks of tin,
All sizes. Once fitted the mask

Was locked to the head,
At the crown, it is said.

You can read of this custom
In a tale of Machado de Assis;

He lived in the slavery days,
Knew how slaves stole pennies

And somehow got intoxicated –
Pennies from their masters.

Are you or are you not,
Gentle reader, reminded

Of twentieth century despots
Who considered freedom of speech

A bad thing for the nation?
Forget about the drink. I think

Some of us nicer people
Could clamp without hesitation

Masks of tin on certain faces,
Gag the mouths of the bullying

Windbags whose abuse
Of the freedom of speech is obscene.

A Spider's Web Caught in Amber

On what plain old beach
was it found, this wonder?

The spider, how fortunate,
must have got away.

We who strive for a mere lifetime
to create a thing of value

envy perhaps the fortunate spider.
A closer look into the pale gold

subdues any grudge: in the web
not one single fly.

Being There

How can it be that of all the old familiar places
That one today assumes,
For no discernible reason, some importance?
Is every one of the places flimsy
Till remembered? Thieves out there in the dark.
In the caravanserai
All of a sudden the blaze of candlelight.

                              From the request bus stop
You step down a gentle slope
And arrive on the patio of a hotel.

On the patio friends are making you welcome.
Soon you will drink. Across a thin strip of beach
Between the new hotel and the ocean
A breeze gets up, violent now and then:
                    So time does expand.
Again the screens of reed are being blown away.

All in all, it was foreign there, but then
                Not spectacularly so.
You did not go back there often, back there
Where it was, where the friends
Rise from their white chairs and smile at you.

Capital of an imperial province,
The ancient city had left few traces there.
Who'd speak of traces? Elsewhere
With every breath you drew from there
A mysterious transparency pulls at you, a fabric
Like diaphans they wove
Not so far away at Byssos,
Worn by the girls Sappho desired and lost.

On Ceasing to Perceive

in memory of Donald Weismann [1914–2007]

Here comes the mood in which I detach myself
From truths I quibbled over only yesterday.
What is hereafter? What is to become of us?
Just when might Malory have tumbled to the English
Responding drily without show of pleasure
And in adversity making light of it.

It was not gravediggers the tradition made of us.
Slowly some sort of adventurers came to be,
Glancing clear and far,
Spirited in the service of their good ships.

Yet into a style it is yourself you steer,
And the feelings are fireworks
For a particular display, a gathering
Moment, and in a different context going dull.
What is it kicks the vivid into a corner
And ushers neutrality into the time it occupied?

Peapod in a trash can such as
Shuntaro saw the aptness and beauty of –
In the absence of what he was ready to perceive
And of the exercise, day in day out, of readiness
To be perceiving it,
Malevolence slips in across neutrality's back.

Malevolence sucks out substance
As the ichneumon fly feeds on a caterpillar,
Proboscis day and night
Pumping the meat of the caterpillar out.
'The men who have been in hand-to-hand combat,'
So Don not long before he died said,
'You can single them out in a crowd.
                        They know something.'

Palingenesis

The very notion must derive from the gaze of some domestic animals. Cow or pig might look you in the eye only for a moment asking why am I, what am I, secreted in this mass, this mélange, of meat and skin.

Then came the cat and the dog. Their gaze might be more protracted, more direct. Even a most wary cat will sometimes shoot you a direct look. The dog will sometimes let his eyes dwell on you, not accusingly, but devotedly.

Only after centuries, perhaps millennia, did the domestic animals come out from the moralistic fog, of punishments and rewards, that people laid around them. But some taboos still persist regarding animals not actually admitted into houses.

Is there one common or garden animal that never did allow its gaze to rest on us, to be interpreted by us? What about the bird? Even the budgerigar, even the talking parrot.

We are told that, with its innate power of discrimination, a cat may even exchange a wink with a person. Prior to that exchange there will have been a careful scrutiny, by the cat, of the person, the familiar-to-be.

The person has to have been, sometimes over long periods, ausculated, sniffed, touched and rubbed, before a cat will risk its first wink. It has to have assured itself that the touch of the familiar equals the password.

The wink, which in an instant shuts and opens the eye, suggests that the cat was heir to a grain of the dust of Empedokles: 'No wise man in his senses will think ... that before they are constituted and after their dissolution mortals are nothing at all.'

A Postcard from Alexandria 1908

The hands clasped
At the base of the spine,
A black hat on the head,
Head and shoulders only
A shadow that clung to a wall
Beyond the lamppost
Where a young man hesitates,
A young man under a straw hat
About to cross the clean
Pale yellow sunlit street
Where horses stand, coaches wait –
Above all, in this suspense
And bath of Alexandrian colour,
Look on again, at the man
Of medium height, walking
Up the street flanking the Bourse,
Ask who could he be,
If not, a man of few words,
A phantom out of Antioch,
Sidonian teller of twilit tales
Taking a stroll in thought,
The pavement under his feet
Hiding skeletons, palaces, temples,
Chests that brim with treasure –
His few words hoist up those
And embody them in Greek
Spiked with the kisses of boys.

Update on the Phrygian Mode

Swinish screams combine with a deafening
Blast of strings picked with electricity,

Flogged bar after bar the same dull beat,
Smeared with drool the stereotypical words

Soon torn apart, their insides flushed out,
In hell there must be multitudes

Which, being there at home, pay up to like it –
Ears being hammered and split,

Synapses snap, neurons sicken of it,
And to cap the triumphs of the age

There is done what was thought unthinkable:
Our devils suck on them and make

Indistinguishable from the pits,
Freakishly costumed, heaven's own harmonies.

Rousseau

That morning came the leaf-blower
Devil's engine levelling all the vowels.

Then the besom swept.
It was like the skimming
Of whole cream, with a ladle,
Off the top of its bucket,

Like Rousseau shushing for mischief
Little French girls.

Little French girls in long dresses.

A Stuffed Shirt

In our dispute relating to rats,
As far as concerns the art
Of their portrayal with heart
And no disparate squeamishness,
We are asked to concede that portrayal
As such would not be a treat.
How should the portrait of a rat
Be wholesome if the rat is not?
And the arts, are they not wholesome?
Never paltry, but impartial?
Even when great, portrayal
Of a rat could exasperate
The wiliest writer: who could fail
To feel in the rat a threat?
Erupting in frat house or Tarrytown,
Won't rats inflict a trauma?
In the theatre you smell a rat:
Can you not trace in every part
The tracks of a rat? Also athletes,
Training cannot eliminate
Two pieces of rat in the rapture
Of racing for trophies and whatnot.
When you are left for dead
There's a chance the rats will eat you.
For reasons possibly obvious
Women fear them greatly.
Like us they are greedy creatures.
Like us they run for shelter.
In the laboratories pampered,
Some rats are even learnèd.
In sewers the world over
Rats wallow in the wet,
And do they or don't they resist
The bacteria they propagate?
For their continued existence,
Like ours, there must be an argument:
You bet your boots any rodent

Attempts at least to be prudent.
Yes, and the white rat with pink eyes
Does befriend the boy who loves it ...
Have I lost the thread? I think not:
Comparative images ratify
Rather than serve to denigrate
Our arbitrator's rationale.
Now can we not congratulate
Ourselves on being, as usual, right?

The Saint Preaches to the Birds

A white cord dangling to the knee
Encircled the bellies in their black habits;

At first the picture shows only two like that.

The figure in front stoops
Over a text of some sort
While the birds have lined up
Composed along five imaginary
Horizontal lines that an artist
Contrived; four or five birds also
Hang about in a little tree
Which slopes toward the fermata
Of the lines. And how polyphonic
Those birds do now look, lined up
Five-fold like the notes in a score,
Silhouetted and slim, his birds.

So hard is he trying,
The saint, to lighten his words ...
To make them strangers to plain speech,
To lift them away from the downpull ...

The entire performance is reprehensible
Even, look out now, the whites
Of the eyes of the preacher and his
Two, yes, now two supporting
Friars, of whom the hindmost, glaring,
Cradles in the crook of an arm
A scarlet book,
                              so who then could stain
The morocco, and how? There's a hat
On the middle figure, whose habit
Sports a snowy girdle of its own.
But all the eyes are amazedly dilated.

The saint, shorter than both others,
Hatless, has to read. Could he not
Have improvised, let fly
His holy words to chime
With the twenty-five songsters
Momentarily perching, silhouettes
Profiled against gold, their background?
They hush but they are versed.

As for what the saint
Did find to say, in gracious Latin,
Was it ever remembered by a bird?
They lined up, willing, to be sure,
Drawn by the saint's etheric
Power, his being their familiar,
Unless the anger whipped him;
Once only could he mimic them,
Levitating in such a posture
As would have scattered them in alarm
Or raised an altogether godless cackle.

Yet even the hindmost figure,
The one who is clutching the book,
The scarlet book, bore witness
To this, a congruence like a seizure,
Incomprehensible, while the saint

Pronounced his apology that the flight
From Paradise had made starvelings
Of the very words it multiplied,
And for the dissolution of Paradise,
Here and now as then.

Rattlesnake

Have you never seen them, in high hats,
the men who chop in three a rattlesnake;
all three sections squirm, the head trailing
a tube of meat squirms up to a mid-
section squirming too, now ugly alien
bait, it threshes under gaping jaws
till the fangs gnaw on it, still squirming,
death sluggish in the bite, no sort of suicide.
Therefore the wisdom of a rattlesnake
must permeate its body, every part of it.
When you talk of heritage, give a thought to this,
also to the high hats and to the rods they wave.

The Moonshine

The providence of women: amazing.
And to picture its origin
In the acumen of a shepherdess.
If she saw, gathering over the hilltops,
A thunderstorm, she set fire to sticks.

See how into her painstaking
Cosmic influences played:
Before the storm could break,
The milk seethed up.
It boiled on the fire of sticks.

It would have curdled, otherwise.
Now the moonshine glided
Through the milk, deep down
It dwelled in the milk, moonshine.

Who but she
Told and retold,
Sometimes blithe, sometimes sobbing,
Of a child being born
For the future of whom
She had not a thing to provide.

In Old Houses

A suspense in every nook,
Odours of mother, of milk,
Of apple baking impregnate
The oak panels, the stone walls.

Quickening walk across the snow
Fresh in the vegetable garden,
Hear the rotting turnip mumble,
Hear the snow squeak.

The dark is complete sometimes.
All the new lights have gone out.
Hear then the stifled laughter
Of children dead of a fever,
Their ghosts still scurry around.

So then the sages, did they mean
That the real worlds came to stay
Instigated by next to nothingness,
And when compulsive magnitudes
Strut, weed has choked the houses.

The clank of armour, the ping
Of crossed rapiers disappeared.
It is fright that you feel only
When through a crack
In a door frame or that of a window
Meaning no harm the wind calls.

Still attached to this dust,
Though absolutely unafraid,
The children, brightest of ghosts,
Go hush when it calls.

Melody

'A muscular contraction
at the mouth, as with laughter,
spread to the eyes, creases
the face.' Sorrow, goodbye,
you took off today in a tune.

And fortified by his escapes,
by rituals, by the diet,
swerves across borders
with a wink at politics,

back in his compromised
country one melody rips
him through
to monstrous grief
and this old Jew caves in.

Roughly Thus was the Beauty
of Certain Facts Delineated

The propeller does not drive the boat,
           it is deceptive,
a most elegant and seductive instigator.

It turns
with a grace, and still the boat
does not begin
to move.

           Attracted by its grace, however,
the water comes and swirls around it. The water
               falls then into the trap,
pushes the boat and carries it along.

And Beckford,
               he built a mansion house,
                   the colossal door
           had wings of bronze;
the porter was a dwarf,
           pressed somewhere with the tip
of his little finger,
               it sprang open with ease.

(after Mallarmé)

What the Hedgehog Said, A.D. 360

In the barbered beard of Julian Apostate
So fetchingly engraved
In relief on a bronze coin
Struck at the mint in Constantinople –
In this bronze barbered beard
There is less of beauty to shiver at
Than in the pizzle of the bull
On the coin's other side,
The pizzle nested in wisps of hair,
Poking out
Beneath the bull's athletic belly,
The bull who walks
By the light of two stars.

The View Back from Whirling Weathervanes

Not everyone loves it when the noise stops.
The volcanoes cooled down overnight.
Now you might see a body of water forming,
Water dark and deathly still,
But no, the pulse of fishes darting everywhere
Travels into your wrist, and a lake
Is turning blue, shorelines touched with rose,
Yellow pears, can those be
The yellow pears again – the water
Reflects their branches; it moves,
Moves, there's no holding it;
Witness the shock as a rippled surface
Has begun to hatch little islands;
On each island a wild copse sprouts,
Soon you'll scent the lime and hawthorn;
Birds flock to each copse and haunt it.
People appear, boats, but stealthily.
Even memories of noise have not arrived here yet.

Seniority

There at a window
Across the open shutters
Finches scribble shadows,
Some scratch at the crossbars,
Others peck at treebark
And here it is again
The Life of a Czar
For him to hear a moment
As he wonders why
For old men it is preposterous
To display any passion
That so hurts and enraptures
The young, any but rage,
Rage and resignation
Since even resignation is a passion
For people grown old to be monsters,
With their wishes unfulfilled,
Their desires unsatisfiable,
And all the music heard.
So much of the wording,
Even then, is doubtful.
Does he resign or renounce?
Things as they are,
Is he seeing them yet?
Stone cold does he see them?

Not Forgotten

All at once the wind
In the wake of the garbage truck,
The wind got up,

Blew two white sheets of paper
In a whirl, each on its own,
Across the parking lot.

At that very instant
Pecking at seeds in the feeder
The nervous sparrow fled,

First beautifully for a blink
Fluttering motionless,
As any sparrow might.

Like the Words Above their Ink

Is anybody there who remembers the Styx?
Summer afternoons
Your love in your embrace
Of course you'll have forgotten it.
Believe it or not, besides,
At Nonacris in Arcadia
You see a little trickle.

It leaks from a rock,
Runs into a basin
And a circular wall
Surrounds the basin
As if to embrace
The sign, the sign a trickle
Even in Cleomenes' time.

Yet they remembered then
The Styx. They believed,
While down the road with blood-feuding
Top tribes could not astonish Sparta,
In Nonacris they believed
That over these waters of silence
We tread unquenched and waltzing.

Friedrich Hölderlin (after 1806)

When out of Heaven

When heavensent a bliss more bright
    Pours down and joy is there for people,
      So that they wonder at things
        Visible, loftier, pleasing,

How sweetly song keeps with it company,
    How truth laughs to the heart in song,
      So is there gladness about a picture –
        Sheep are passing along the path now,

A parade that goes almost into twilit woods.
    What's more, meadows are spread with green
      Pure as that of the heathland
        Which in its usual way is not far

From the dark wood. There, on the meadows too
    These sheep linger. The tops of hills
      All around, stark heights, are spread
        With oak trees and sparse fir.

There, where ripples of the stream are lively,
    So that someone coming along the path
      Will be glad to look on, ascends the gentle
        Form of the hills with vineyards.

True, the steps go up among the vines
    And down where the fruit tree presides
      And fragrance dwells on the wild hedge
        Where violets, unseen, are sprouting.

Waters run trickling down and a gentle
    Murmuring is to be heard the whole day;
      But all of an afternoon in the neighbourhood
        The villages are hushed and still.

Remembering White Chickens

I might have believed her
    A misfit, she crouched
And let red gravel
    Slip between her fingers.

I might have said red hair,
    Tall bony brow, eyes periwinkle.
Then up she awkwardly stood
    And yapped, yapped without reason.

Down she had sat on the bench,
    A companion beside her;
I might have watched the lake glitter,
    Fishes and dogs and canoes

Make headway in the water.
    But I only said she stooped again,
Hands picking at red gravel
    On which so much depended.

On the Eve of Independence Day

Unimaginably no fishes
   lax in the glittering water
     stuck their heads up
       for her, as she passed
         canoeing with indolence,
           to greet them. Not
             intrusive at the time,
               herself at the bow, her guy
                 steering, graciously she spoke
                  to strangers on the shore:
              And how are you? Do
          have yourselves a nice day now
        and happy holidays tomorrow.
      On she went, over
    the glitter, slowly, slowly
   digging her paddle in,
  calling so the stranger
 heard how she spoke
her mind that day: Hello folks, hello there!

Then

Singing at once all three:
Hoopoe, nightingale, blackbird,
Don't believe a word of it.

       Perched, yes,
On the lip of a canyon,
       I heard them,
The intervals between their calls
Obeyed no measure.
         Only the first I saw:

When from the top of its rock
Which housed an ancient broken chapel
The hoopoe sang
Hopopop hopopop

Its crested head went up and down,
Made miniature, for the likes of us
At hand, tumultuous vistas.

Jabbering east of there, zealots out to kill;
Miseries between their fangs
Munched on the faces of children.

Small wonder they would say in Egypt then
Of its grandmother:
'She created the light with her feathers,
Produced the wind with her wings.'

The Four Curios

Was interfusion once the word
For sedimentation in the galleries
Of consciousness? A trickling
Down?

                    But I do treasure
A silver shilling of a star-crossed monarch,
The book from France signed on the flyleaf
By poet and artist in 1922,
Of Norfolk flint a willowleaf arrowhead,
This oval Inca pot –
What do these useless implements interfuse?

The hours do load them,
The hours are exerted in them
To fill their orbits, trickling in

Through feelings uniquely I
Still tilt over them.

              Now they age
Imperceptibly. Exotic
And picturesque or not,
Rare and valuable or not,
Hardly fingered by today –

              Yet a happy sight of them,
Or touch, appears
To interfuse a doubt, the ground
Collapsing in a cave –
Gone for keeps with so much junk
The times when they surfaced, times
That planted scars on them, for veneration.

Do not now look back on them
Unless the look springs on
Even to perpetuate a puny comedy
Of getting by. Void, hallo, positively
Filling with new time, feelings deepen,
Earth turns, from the shadow, out of danger.

So count the days, years unremembered, dull
Times in bewilderment, but hear a certain cry,
From an eternity that never was,
For their safe custody after mine.

Seniority (2)

(from the gnome)

Look out, up, on,
Look in, back
Of beyond, look
Nothing but what,
Else an edge, of
Crater, is cold
– Moon put out –
But thunder, hero,
Whose mass?

From body
Worm peeks.
Take and drop it.
Take heart.
Of being again
Body, dread
And delighting
Clear heart,
Wag head.

Then remorse?
Then old lusts?
At whose expense
Cast out the lot?
What, what
The devil is left?
Haply the weak
At the knees
Bless, are blest.

The Halving of France

Winter night, with jobless wives,
They combed the supermarket
For food they could afford.
Stout wives, you, also skinny ones,
And blithe or anxious,
Must load your chariots
With sweet potato, cauliflower.

Soon killed in the first war,
Her brother saying he believed
All of it, Isabelle Rivière
Thought she saw, being clarified,
The supernatural world
Like a garden when the moon rose
Slowly over a wall.

Feuilleton 10: Rather Vague About Vienna

Brought on by some lugubrious and squashy
Orchestral music by Siegfried Wagner,
A torrent of Austria came upon me,
Specifically the scene in Vienna –
With, I allow, Benedictine and Brandy.

Then brushing the booze aside,
Silencing the music in my head,
I could hear steel nibs at work
Or fountain pens. Trakl in a tavern,
And simpering Altenberg in his café,
Hofmannsthal of the golden intelligence
At work on radiant sentences
Concerning Griechenland. It was
Stefan Zweig whispering to himself
Essays on fighting the Demon down amid

His collection of autographs. Wittgenstein
Had nothing to say yet. Karl Kraus tootled,
However, on his tremendous old trombone,
Or loaded a critique into a harpsichord.

For all of these minds,
Asleep or awake,
Were married to music.
Then doglike all
As best they could
Shook off the wet of cliché.

My Raft of the Medusa had to be drifting
Downstream. In my trance
Inequality of the races, imperial soldiery
Holding the Montenegrins down, the times
Perplexed, were mud, whole peoples driven
Deep into it, in atavistic villages
Mud muffled the howl for vengeance.

Closer I heard in Petropolis, Brazil,
The pen of Stefan Zweig, with equanimity,
Scratching still; I could not make out
The sounds of suicide, his
And his wife's: two pistol shots? –
While on the doors in Vienna
Knuckles were knocking –
A gurgle? Might they together
Have hanged themselves?

                    (The Zweigs ...?
                    (Petropolis ...?

Epilogues

Old School Remembered

Where girls never sang I heard a certain music
And am again in that manorial dining hall at school,
Organ pipes climb the gallery opposite, and here –
A table strewn with records, seventy-eights –
Delius, Brahms, Sibelius, Mussorgsky.
On an afternoon we looked beyond our histories,
Ransacked the albums, heard the music grow.

A melody chanced to mix in my perception with
A boy whose husky speech, laughter, nonchalance,
His walk perhaps, had made me love him.
Who now, out there, can hum the prelude
By César Franck that I compounded with the boy
So fiercely that, six decades later, hearing it
My heart quickening sends through me a silly thrill.

Years have passed, gone for ever –
And for a little while the thing retraces you,
A craving, touches that were clandestine,
Separations, to the music, anguish all the way,
In utter ignorance, to the immaterial.
Dead now, younger then, he might also have known,
Before too late, the enormity of a passion.

A force that models the prelude drew me to him,
Husky voice, chipped front tooth, skin
Grainier than eggshell, not at all feminine,
Shoulderblades gleaming, provocative, from the bath.
That strain again, and chasms in the skull
Release wild, wild flocks of sentiment.

How vaguely we forms grope past one another.
But love that was not reckless was not love.

In Memory of the Great Edward FitzGerald
(1809–83)

1

Reddened at a dinner table,
Scanners of the fashion magazines,
These young and old dependable business girls,
When they wave into the air their elbows
And in concert laugh so shrill,
Ow, what an exhalation of stale fish.

Near the illustrious but vanished
Temple of Dionysus
At Teos on the coast of Caria, still
There is water, cold and fresh, to drink
From a subterranean spring.
There is also a tin cup on a chain
To be lowered into the spring.
From very deep down there is a whisper.

A mouthful of water anywhere
Must contain a long time.
Gods, fill my cup with wine.

2

To Fanny Kemble, April 1879: He'd read
Of Peggotty again, and was wonderstruck
When Peggotty discovered her and threw
Over the lost girl's face a handkerchief,
Then took her in his arms, as if forever.

That winter also he had often heard
(As earlier, the seawind plunge in the Chimney)
The tolling of the Funeral Bell;
Springtime as it was in his Woodbridge garden,
'Daffydowndilly and Hyacinth,' how difficult
A time they'd had of it for growing.

No, it was not on his mind that the machines
Might take our speech away from us.
His hurt eyes straining close to the folio,
By no means the last thing he heard:
Though two were dead, his one blackbird sang,
Sang, he wrote, 'across the Funeral Bell.'

History of the Hat

(*variation on a prose poem by Jean Follain*)

The stranger who found there
A welcome, there in a house
On the street of a village
Where the cobblestones shone,
Summer haycarts over them bumped,
And cattle would pass the winter,
Forgot his hat, an everyday hat
But decorous, and it was kept
Respectfully, never thrown away,
Never sold at a brocante,
Accordingly in the event
Of the stranger's return he'd even
Have found it brushed and clean,
But return he didn't, so the hat
Vanished one day into the mind
Of a boy and the boy as a man
When he later lay, sleepless
In lodgings where once had been
Another village not long since
Ruined in one of the wars,
Saw it afloat in the dark, saw
Exactly the same hat in mid-air,
And amazed as he was
At its having absorbed him once,
At his remembering it perfectly,

Later he told of what he'd seen,
The crown high or low, the brim
Wide or not, soft or stiff
Its actual fabric, make of it
What we will, with invention
Limited only by the aptitude
Of hats for heads, by a sense
Of utility, by quality, style
And colour embracing the object,
Freely ourselves now we float it.

For Want of an Axiom

What an antique air had the almost effaced sundials, with their
moral inscriptions, seeming coevals with that Time which they
measured, and to take their revelations of its flight immediately
from heaven, holding correspondence with the fountain of light!
                              Charles Lamb, *Essays of Elia*

Old Dunwich / In Writing, Memory

'… for want of old Dunwich
Whose ruined Tower I saw from sea,
And me seasoned with Salt,
Spray, Wind, and the Sun …' not

Misremembered the legible words
Stretch
But less far back than 1880,
Call to mind the flapping orange
Mainsails of the herring luggers,
Cold Lowestoft days, little boys
Frightened then by nothing,
We blew on freezing fingertips, stuttered Latin,
Scooped chunky porridge from its bowl,
And now the Tower,
                 Aquitaine, the prince
Had abdicated, in his boots a twilight man
Crunched along the beach of pebbles,
A woman is
                 'washed ashore
After the Storm, she clung
Still to the child in her arms.'

(Edward FitzGerald, letter of July 16, 1880)

Reminiscence Remembered

They drew their water from a holy well;
Two rounded lips of stone and a trickle
Of freshest water from a deep laid spring,
That's what he waited for; that water
Eventually filled the family's zinc pail.

Grandpa is only telling you, boy,
Word for word what the daft old man said
And I remembered.

At a distance, he told me, where dunes
Had rolled their shifting shapes along,
An ancient church had been discovered.
Now there were outlines only,
And lumps of dressed stone. Attractive
To him, in many ways, a boy of ten,
Were the graves. Discovered weeks before,
Vertebrae came from them, slivers of shinbone,
Small curving fractions of skull.

And which way did it ever shine, a lighthouse,
For captains of cargo ships he saw by day
Creeping from Ophir on the long horizon?

Sometimes a gale blew off the Atlantic
With such fury that the tents fell down.
If it blew at night its roar
Frightened him only a bit, it was funny
The way it made everything flap.

The wind ruffled up the sea, drove inshore
Thongs of slimy seawrack, or a shoe,
Somebody's pocket-watch. There were dead gulls
On the tideline, a porpoise dead and smelly,
Rarely a globe of glass, dabs of paint on it,
For stars or flowers, white stripes circled
At a right angle the circumference. He said

The tideline where you went scavenging
Was a silent historian of our resolves.

The holy well, the skullbones, the deposits
Had no roots or consequences then.
Nor had the huge rock offshore, still there surely,
With its twin wings peaking
And smothered in cormorants, suggested yet
That of many things two, like right and left,
Jut from the deep at degrees of tension
To co-exist, or to wrestle.

His Daddy in shorts, replacing his pipe
Unlit between his teeth, had told
Another story. Fish or sausage
Sizzled in mother's old black frying pan.
Of the holy water from his pail
She made cocoa, hot in blue tin cups.

He twittered on, never querulous, about
A rope (none too taut) across a gulf
That's spoken of – and still hushed about –
As history. The well, the bones, bygones,
Properties trodden over, but they were things
Blessed or taken for granted in their time.

But of time, he groaned, it is deep
Pools of blood in the purposes of madmen.

How long is there to go before benign
Animism has been stolen from the species?

Even squinting then into his memory
Of one or two such things, he saw that nobody
Might ever sniff the holy at first flush.
But at a distance it is holier still, he said,
Because you found the time to make it so.
To subdue the false, the foul, the fatuous,
He told me, fragile instruments is what we are.

In the American Park

There by the riverside, making my way back
To the old pecan trees, I was admiring
Her free and easy walk, fine rustic features,
When from the far side of a stream in shadow
Came through trees two sharp voices calling.

Strangers ourselves, in passing I asked
Isn't it strange to hear from there
Two Spanish voices. They are Chinese,
The lady said. So much the stranger.

Hobbling on I meet
Three marvellous little girls, the children
Of that lady. Clothed
In cottons blue and white and black
They were collecting the last pecans.

Making jokes and chattering, they dawdled
With unpretended grace and interest in the shells,
Showed me how to jump on them, to ascertain
If nut meat was inside or no nut. For miles around –

The sky quite blue, sunshine in December,
It really must be so that great delight
At feminine presence makes docile the mind:
Into a moment's oblivion scooted all
The bullies and charlatans, stuffed shirts, weirdos.

The Murmur of Erasmus

Not everyone shaken by a memory
Can for long enough shrug off
These spectres of a world blown up –

Not everyone finds time to care
For long enough to recall a memory
In its bare bones:

The doors of glass fly open
On a garden complete with its round pond,
A bed for every five rose bushes;

Round the pond, with one white rose opening,
Beds all set in radiant order,
Concerted as a wind quintet.

On flagstones the pied wagtails,
The little clicking of their claws:
Old summers, young skin took to the warmth

That crept into Norfolk now and then,
And a lawn freshly mowed this morning
Renders up air airier for the scent of green.

Anxieties of algebra,
They never entirely quit
Though they could not always torment

The boy who stole the secret of birds, the witness
Rapt in their strut, in the long tail-feathers
Wagging as quickly as tongues.

These tens of thousands of years
Unmade, at risk, even if life itself
Has no object but to be and to be opening

Beyond the social construct. Zealots
Now calculate only to destroy; stunted bullies,
Where great questioners could not, will not mend the world.

Would fiends, even then, being cognitively
Gingered, find refreshed their muscle
Gladly to make do with mere humanity?

Contrariwise, too, electric speeding keys
To knowledge in such temporal abundance
Do not deepen but subjugate understanding.

What if the Great Memory should rise up
And wash the world
With a fine storm of algebraic equations.

How Blacktop Burned Beethoven

Blacktop, the darker boy, Trinity chorister,
Seldom relished meals, said he liked 'bits;'
Poking a bonfire of hollyhock stems,
Branches of pear, branches of apple,
Old seventy-eights of melting shellac,
On red labels a dog sat, 'sag' he'd say
And dramatise it, there, by the wall
At the end of the garden, smoke
Spiralling up to where the bombs
Were going to fall from, 'sa-a-g' he'd say
And stretch the word as it rose from the action.

Overheard in the Agora

Why this pernicious craving for noise with drums,
With saucepans, scramble of yelling multitudes?
I will not make light of such matters,
But what do men go to battle for,
If not to make noises and to hear them?
While the arrows hiss and swords
Whack on shields, they pretend
It's all about things of immense benefit –
Hunting grounds, markets, glory.

With other animals it is not so,
Unless our wolves are an exception.
The elephant, such a wise creature, trumpets
Never unless enraged; the dog
Or horse, amiably
With yap or whinny they pronounce the silence.

Watch out, for the noise of two
Is swallowed up in a third's greater din.

Might the gods have pent in men's minds
A foul congestion – their own default,
A block that, for a time,
As walking, so Aristotle insisted,
Loosens the bowels, noise alone can undo?

And the louder the noise, the fouler the congestion?

Leo III Iconoclast

Is anything at all actually paralleled,
Even if orthography makes it seem so?
I was thinking of the shock to nightingales,
Shy-come as one prodigious hayseed called them,
Shy-come the first arriving nightingales,
Hearing so much as the softest
Footfall in their spinney
All hushed 'as if no bird were anywhere,'
And as the Patriarch Germanus hushed prophetically
When in a decorated antechamber
The emperor spoke his name and purpose,
So for fifty years what could anyone do –
The eyeballs of saints galore going up in smoke,
At night among fig trees a woman buries a picture,
Invisible to boys the features of God's mother?
It was later that the villagers
Heard and spoke of new-come nightingales,
For they believed they began to sing for them.
That is how it was in those old villages.

Daphne

> *Everything gone except her grace, her shining.*
> Ovid, *Metamorphoses*, 1,552, trsl. Rolfe Humphries

Silly as it is to fuss like this,
How come a land has locked me in?

There was that rush, of air, of sea,
To take me, to draw my float
Into any little room it happened to choose,
            Air no shadowy medium,
Sea sufficient to itself.

Watch out,
The moment this year is up I'll migrate again.
A fond hope cannot be unreasonable today.

First, to shake off this husk,
This brittle husk that prickles me. My quintet
Of senses will perform heroically then.
Images I dwell on with a passion
Might be less intractable.

                              I have done with begging them
To loft me, freely swimming
Into the hollow cones of tufa stone once more,
 Into ancient scented atmospheres.

I should look to the ancestors:
You dodge the sungod only to be upstaged
By smouldering stacks of damp straw. First
Facility bloats the arts, then it slackens them –
A putrid conceit, and octopus ego, have stuffed
The dreck of the world into them.

Target then what might become, but loop
Your pebble round the patch
Of yellow touched
Aptly by the painter into 'A View of Delft'.

If there is turbulence, remain reasonable.

Listen, go greatly mad that all
Terror broke loose, with worse to come,
But study loving still.

                    Pray that whatever
Blew incomprehension away will show
In a shell of light
                    Earth whole and needful,
Histories in their husks not bogus,
Peace no nest of living worms.

Happening

What if no monk had been walking by
As the boy Goya with a stick of charcoal
Portrayed a pig on a wall in Fuendetodos? –
As if Demosthenes could happen
To have put into his mouth
Not a pebble but a grasshopper.

Vasily Kalinnikov Composes

Truly real is this alone,
Tavern room, crepuscular,
A lantern on the table,
Wick half up half down,
A tune to scorch the paper.

★

Crimea, let me not die in you.
Time is for music, on with it.
Beyond my semiquavers Caucasus
Is not real at all at all;
Days of shooting, now and then,
A tired topic of conversation.

★

Lantern on a wooden table,
Tin ribs cast a cage of shadows.
Here's vodka in its bottle,
Swirls of papyrossi smoke,
A surge of air crests afresh,
Welcomes a biting whiff of piss.

★

Truly this alone, a room
Crepuscular but warm,
Lantern flame, and no soot, my nose
Savours the kerosene, my music –

Flow deep, strings, your surges
Waylaid, no, but lightened
By these two notes, close-knit,
A silver bell keeps pinging –

Fire, from our essential fuels,
For souls afloat, naked
And thin, craving space to bloom in,
Being down here, being barbarous
Give warmth it must, second by second.

(V. K., 1866–1901)

Variation on Orhan Veli Kanık's Poem about Listening to Istanbul

Then he was listening for life
To the shadow crawling heavily,
Yes heavily toward him. He shut,
He shut, he really did, his eyes,
Meaning to listen even more intently

To the calls of the masons in vacant lots
Measuring everything out already;
To the hammering from the dock,
To the lisp of gulls' wings as they passed
The open window that now seemed
To squeeze out the last and future light.

What was now the value of knowledge,
With such colours and stratification?
He was listening for life,
But then what was it
But a twitter, but a pang
At the time lost, the time wasted.

He was listening for life.
He had closed his eyes.
The smoke of feasting in his lungs,
Of feasting long ago, never yet
Exhaled, how bitter it now tasted.

For life he listened then,
And the great fish-filled net
Was being winched to the surface,
Without one sprat for him,
Not one sprat. This town was his time:
For how long would he be missed?

Hold out, if he so could, a moment longer,
His fret would be emptied out, his devil
Quit with a hiss. Out of nowhere
Came fullness,
All was not lost, on himself, meaning
Nobody else, without pride, he had counted,

Giving his utmost, not squandering it,
Even while listening
                          Not for the harmonies
Compounded by the spheres, not for the grunt
Of griffins hauling, immense,
Their heraldic limousine; for look,
She walks in with her smile and the teapot.

He's listening still
For the rustle of her dress,
And rustling it accompanies
The completion of her walking.

Two Poems of Love

1

Another Slave Girl Lost
    (after a motif in Po Chü-i)

The caged bird owes no allegiance,
Or so the old old Chinaman told himself.
She owed him nothing but a lick of love.
It must once have been thrilling to be free.

She did fool around, O several times;
To cage her he'd have been the more a fool –
When immemorial anguish struck again,
His fine frenzy swept away precaution.

If another one flits in,
He'll cage her good and proper.

Then she can make light even of her career,
And if they feel a freedom, sweet it is
Most mordantly whenever it compels …

Is this logic clean or clean off-kilter?
He'll tell himself and wish that he was listening:
You'll make the same mistake and you'll be right.

2

Damn the Tango

What did it   mean to say
How should you   dance to it
Feel how it   agitates

Who can do   steps so quick
Why does she   grip his neck
Should he just   let her go

Now they're both   holding tight

Now she e   ludes his grip
Now he will   bend her back
But she kicks   up her heels

Why must this   all go on
Why is the   room so dark
O look a   gain, the grace
The fiddles   mew and squeak
The bando   leon groans

Now I re   member her
How we were   lovers once
She's sixty   four at least
Over the   hill but hot
Stuff at the   tango too

Zamoscz

Who is she that looketh forth as the morning … ?

Song of Songs, 6, 10

More precisely than I
Remember the story he told
Of a garden that grew
By the fortress, he pictured
The little gentile hunchback girl.
A general's daughter? Something like that.

They come to me often,
Approach me (more truly said),
That girl in the garden, the Jewish
Boys who could glimpse her
Through cracks in the fence.
By customs restricted, their lives

Must often have seemed suspended
And small. Ugly, fat or wizened or squat,
Swarthy also most of the Jews, and gentiles
Were few and far in Zamoscz.
By custom and codes for the doing
Of most things, or not, they were netted,

And the sight of the gentile girl
Who was a little hunchback
Was also forbidden – discovered
Hanging about for a glimpse of her
Through a crack in the fence,
The boys would be whipped.

Who told of her (nobody else did)
Came soon to be perplexed, even tormented
About life and reasons for it, purposes,
And about reasons for death.
The Enlighteners did not prevail.
Enlightenments only told you the coat to wear.

But long, long after
A glimpse, one only perhaps,
For I cannot recall precisely,
She still dwelled on his mind
And haunted the stories he wrote,
And the garden grew in his mind.

Look this up in a memoir of his:
We would sneak up to the fence
For a glimpse of her.
She might have been picking flowers,
A little gentile hunchback girl,
She might be reading a book.

In good faith, hump, garden and all,
Memory found her a living soul.
Soon with a slaughter machine
Others tore us apart. How should memory match
Evil organised with chimneys?
                              The singular
Bygone denied, death-squads walk away.

Alt-Hermannstadt / Bukovina

1

From door to door the boobies went
        rapping, kicking,
                plucking the people out.
Every one an individual:
        Had she made jam today?
    Had he been to school?
                Was grandpa incontinent?
Stuffed into trucks (some helped
        and stretched out hands to hoist
    The bony girls and babies in),
                they went for ever off.

These arches, tunnels, now
                arcades, for shopping,
        and the square they circle,
                commodious, homely
Attic and Doorstep, red, tiled,
                pitched roofs not far
    from clouded hills, the domed
Church Tower sunlit – smoked meat to smell –
                no sign of what
        the boobies did, no sign indicative
of their routine marks these materials.

2

But how come they did, the others,
                just what they were told?
      Was obedience the thing
                from immemorial time appointed?
      Frightened, they still hoped
            it might not be too bad.
If liberty's a gift
      you take it as it comes,
            and nobody, for sure,
                has cause to murder me.
I'll find fresh geraniums.
I'll pot them in the porch.

3

You gaze across the roofs,
      moonlit, or rained upon,
            shut they are, shut mouths,
with chins drawn down they smirk.

Huge worms of malice, can it be,
      perforate the matter we become.
Since then the very body
           was made a booby weapon.
Hear music warm the market square;
Of agonies that folly perpetrates
           none do likewise.

Lonesome Toper, Busy Barmaid

Not tonight in desperation, Jacqueline,
                But I would ask,
Catching your attention as you fly past,

      ★

By events, by people
Trodden down, from under the heel,
Who might still squeak?

      ★

       So it is
When the flood of shit smashes up against
Cliffs your little watch-tower shivers on;

      ★

       So it feels
While you read, read of wild Russian violets,
Of colts trotting up to you, across meadows,

      ★

       Of quail, of duck
There, believable, in the matted canes,
Even of old small–bore shotguns –

      ★

       Surely not
Everything ground between the millstones
Turns into stars; the barely palpable

      ★

Things can persist,
Coming up out of their scourged skin
Things long gone recur, you tell me,

★

In the wistful, wistful smile that flits
Across the Polish woman's face at supper,
Gasps for breath in their voices

★

When children count, dispute, tell
Their stories,
Make their promises. The turpitudes

★

Are not inscrutable,
Killings of whoknowswho could have been,
Who knows, averted, even the chill

★

Somebodies who rule the roost
Can be, comes their moment, for that moment,
Cool heroes. All the bases shift,

★

The moon's angle makes the lighting change,
And a scarlet sundown will not signify
For stage shepherds, even,

★

Evil. Myself I tell, doom
Will strike. Could ever the invention
Of a style have extirpated our crudity?

★

They are shopping for carcasses these days,
Recrimination, acrimony
Seethe in their cooking pot. It counts

★

Not now as sin to show
To the light of day blood coiled up in skin
But still untamed, still rippling, Jacqueline.

Like Heart's Desire

The bars to the gate of the castle are cold;
Whenever night begins
See in the walls so many windows,
How they light up, one after another,
Blue and lemon and crocus also.

★

Country house, lighthouse, court house,
Or a fort gains ground in its maze of huts,
For sure the rules of perception
Shape the castle never quite the same; watch,
And but for the lamps it is otherwise again.

★

The fragility of life rather deeply worrying him,
Through huge rooms the butler Robert
Loves to pace, as night begins;
He roams with his box of matches,
Long sulphur matches;
He lights the paraffin lamps,
Docks a wick if that is called for.

★

Slight of build, shoulders narrow and sloping,
But not so old as to be almost invisible,
Seriously the genius Robert goes
With quiet tread about his butler's duties.

★

Seldom seen is Robert:
Mornings at the table where he polishes
All the tall glass cylinders,
Nobody could be certain where he sits;
Nor is the prose of the huge interiors to be seen.

★

Hold the cold bars, hold and watch,
Watch the splendour, how it happens;
How tangled darkness is,
Now how trim when Robert passes,
How homely all the windows are
When like heart's desire, one by one,
Wicks do light up, every lamp glows
With a brave trembling flame.

(*Schloß Dambrau, Upper Silesia, Autumn 1905*)

Sonnet of Irreconcilables

With an audible smile the announcer confides to us
That Mozart is sensuous: 'In fifteen minutes
Alfred Brendel will show our listeners how.'

Soloists perish fighting radicals in the mountains.

Next she recites an anecdote and notes her liking of it.
Her time is managed, spurts of chatter come on cue.

What are we doing to ourselves, cheapening
The sensitive words, or statistics of bloodshed?

There goes the wheelbarrow stacked with body-parts.

While music is intangible, 'breath,'
As Rilke felt, 'breath of statues,' and while
Bodies respond to it without sight or taste,

While its mobility thrills my temporal brain,
Brute force crawls subtly into the speech of a culture.

Figure of Relation, the Part of Speech

Stumble into the rift tomorrow carves from time.
                    In diverse notes relation
Discovers mistily today's configuration:
                    All but forgotten
The khaki flock. And so midwinter 1944
Brings to Brussels, straight from battle,
Four hundred soldiers on a 48. Dog-tired
They file into the Hotel Albert.

Incomprehensible the mockingbird, in April
He sings for his delight; into the open
Showers of notes jet,
                    Agitate the shopping centre,
                    Colour distant hills cobalt blue.

Rapider than a piston
The tongue must school from the throat
Quick liquid breathing in one beam of song.
Nothing remarkable in the chill church

But an altar lit by a fat candle. In the nave
A column is flecked emerald and azure;
A rare ray of sun passed through a window.

Here for the soldiers the faithful pray;
Over whitecaps their various murmur
                Wings it and cheers the soldiers,
Who remember the faithful and think of them fondly.

Soon the muck is being washed
From bodies that got away with it this time.
              Before lights-out, together
All sing the top song of that wartime.

A Parable for Rembrandt

How beautifully Fausta the lithe black she-cat
Flew from the floor to assume on the desk top
The posture of an ancient leathern flask.

Still as still can be the black and lithe cat
Sat beside the lamp and did not topple it.
Gazing through the panes of glass the cat

Could watch an oblong tube of seeds for birds:
How hotly that stalker wanted a finch, wanted
To be crunching one of them, quick as a breath.

Across matter, so, the invisible inscribed itself,
Birds' heads nervily swivelling, birds
Perched and flitting to and from the tube.

Stillness, what a stillness of the cat.
Sometimes you wonder when the focus comes
Finally to rest on a small intervening fly,

The fly making an agitation flood the scene,
Wanting out, finding no way, dabbing
Its adhesive footsoles on a glass Alaska –

Such a pedestrian the cat perhaps forgot it?
No, focus sharpens on what intervenes and phases
Out the fruits of sunlight in the remote tube.

Now of squabbling birds that peck at them,
Of sunflower seeds inside the thing outside
Not a sign: the focus rested on the fly.

Banality Overwhelming

Still it twists the heart if you retreat
To 1829, in Paris, on a boulevard:
Piaf's progenitor
Turning the handle of his barrel-organ,
A musician sang,
And for the lyric a song-sheet spelled out
Passers-by paid so little – took their time,
And sang with others.

A sunny day, light's embrace and Edward
FitzGerald only twenty then;
After eighty years, much the same scene,
And Guillaume Apollinaire wondered about it;
Still sooner Stevenson whose
Wanderers halting at
'Some green-embower'd house play their music,
Play and are gone on the windy highway.'

Béranger dead and gone, who never knew
He carried a torch for the popular culture;
Whose worst nightmare never was the song
Become an uproar of the collective man.

Reiterating antique measures that you trash,
What might you make of this,
Noisemakers of now? Unless you go with the flow
Down the drain, kiss goodbye to money.

You Did Not Wake Up

The image of this wide stone staircase
Is riper now than in an old dream.
Down you go.
A subterranean bazaar? A cistern?
And where are they, the various people?
Discern through altitudes of shadow
How fan-vaulting intricately freights the roof.

You did not wake up in a sepulchre.

A Dainty Shopper

Eyes glued to the guide book
I scud over the dust
Of a few forgotten peoples.

Tell you what:
From their cups I never drank,
From their platters I ate not a crumb,
Of stories on their lips
I never heard a word.

Eyes glued to the guide book
I wanted I know not what.
Shining articles in various materials
Took my guided eyes, instant by instant

164

Often by surprise,
Often to the thing
I had not known I wanted.

Eyes glued to the guide book
I trod across a few fond beliefs.
What could it mean to me,
You know, the deep believing?
Distance must detain the object of it

Or belief misguided
Crashes among commodities; always
One and then the next I wanted. I
Suppose I was manipulated. My desires,
Tricked by novelty, became prosaic.

(There, in the bankrupted butcher shop,
Strings of sausages still hung down,
Rats were crawling in and out of them.)

As for empires and their expansion,
Let me have my meat and my potatoes.

A house, not spacious, with a wooden porch,
A trumpet vine growing around the posts,
Good rough neighbours on each side, conveniences
Enough, water always fresh, and wine –
I do not ask for nothing, or too much.

Of Sympathy

Help our decay, / Man is out of order hurled ...
George Herbert (1633)

As age and adversity in Africa made
More merciful a strict saint and magistrate,

Every moment possibly still
To wake and walk is good, to visit

Gutters where not one bomb awaits,
To sniff the Mexican plumtree flowers,

And know then that one day you'll even miss
(A passing thought, and inconsequential)

The rush of traffic, its persistent din,
Rumble and beep from the construction site –

So seldom hereabouts, after sunrise,
Does a summer breeze not blow cool,

And the bringing of discord not attract sympathy;
No matter how the grammar of it goes,

Wake now again, if hoarfrost grips
Do not shrink; while sense responds,

No screens to warp it, reality
Giving itself in the street, not quite lost –

The river rambles on, very ancient,
Whispering to itself of the hidden waterfall,

And the captain stops, for he perceives
So far away its source, on such a day.

The Shorter Breath

Comes with age, the stroke,
When swimming, is laboured,
The poem in its pea-shooter
A pellet, waits for weeks;
Finally fired
It falls short. No matter
Nothing is resolved. Time –
The concertina at full stretch.

The Night

for Geoffrey Hill

Rolling sometimes over velvet
The night comes on,
And through an open door
In they stream,
Not for company,
Stinging bugs and
Silly defenceless ones,
Greedy for light,
For blood sealed up in skin.

And every day still they happen,
Simple things: the bee
Brings no basket,
No whole flowers. It broods over them,
One by one, extracting
Force, the spirit, say
Quintessence, which bees eat,

But for the likes of us, if Montaigne
Is to be believed, their own,
Entirely their own, the honey,
Sweet and good, not any longer
Thymian nor Marjolaine.

On the Road from Van Kure to Urga

Spring came everywhere in immense Mongolia;
Cranes performed their weird courtship dance,
On the backs of the little imourans
Yellow larks rode, pecking parasites out,
Warning with a whistle when an eagle came near.

A splendid beast the killer baron's
White camel. Squatting on the hump,
What a large view the rider had.

Demons haunt certain mountains, monasteries
Among flaming lakes were fortified. On roads,
In many makeshift towns, massacre, murder,
Bolsheviks, White officers, Cossacks, the Chinese:
The lash and backlash of revolution drove
Through men's minds insane
Interpretations of chaos.

Nature does for life every favour. Nature
Dissipates death with snow and dust.

Still, butchered,
Strewn across our trail, in heaps beside it,
Hundreds of young Chinese soldiers.

Some showed the ghastliest wounds from swords.
Faraway the grandmothers
Hoped for word of them.

(Ferdinand Ossendowski, 1921)

Kangaroo

A kangaroo tamed is a matter of make-believe,
Yet they can be pictured so –
Expansive householder, the male on his haunches,
His spouse, a sturdy person, her baby
Sagely peers from the handbag, no,
A pouch of fur that brackets her belly.

All over the outback they go hopping,
For miles and miles. Night coming on,
Who knows, the day's hopping done,
They congregate and share experiences.

Though not mute they must have invented
A body-language. In what their quiddity
Spells out, in circles drawn by custom,
Nature hoops and drives them. Bounding

Over obstacles with a levity
We might dream of, travelling distances
Descried by us in images born of speech,
They do not reflect. Their heads, accordingly,
Harbour no eschatology. This

Flea's Jehovah, emblem of Being,
Inconvenience its only Antibeast, aeons gone
Its demiurge dreamed of a universe in stitches.
If it comes too close for comfort,
You run.

Belshazzar

In Daniel's book the original report
Has been filed. At his feast
Only the king saw the hand
Writing on the plaster of the wall.
                    Only the king,
Not the dinner guests. Only sensationalists
Portray them horrified, scrambling
Bug-eyed all over one another.
Only the king's hair stood on end.

                    The report has been,
Even then, misconstrued. The report –
After all, it happened long ago,
People had not yet invented matters of fact –
Hinted broadly that in the king's vision
Memory spoke and authority no longer.

                    Interior palace walls
Were tiled, not plastered. Besides,
By morning the kingdom had been destroyed –
For months conspirators planned insurrection.

And the king, while showing
Ceremonially his person in the city
Had caught sight of a graffito
Scrawled in Babylonian on a plastered wall.

The king's attention wandered from feasting,
Suddenly he remembered
The power of those few words against him,
And 'his countenance was changed

And the joints of his limbs were loosened,'
For he saw afresh a hand that wrote on plaster
Shrinking him to a lightweight in the scales.
Now the hand was there, close to the candlestick.

Variation on Prose by Rudolf Kassner

I have caught in a swan's eye a look
Of annoyance – a look unlike
A viper's, not vengeful;
And the eye of a hawk, the socket
Sloping down on its way back,
Even has an air of joylessness.

★

The slender triangle laid on its back
And the dark ring set in its apex
Produce the look. It is not hostile.
The annoyance is not aimed at you or me.

★

How emptied of swan they did swim along,
The swans, even in their motion
Musical instruments made of glowing plumage,
And the water placid – might this one startle
To have been transfigured, so,
A mirror of perfection, self-contained?

★

Then beauty is not looking out for anyone.

★

That look of annoyance had preoccupied
The eyes of beautiful expensive courtesans.
Yet they hid their contempt
Of clients with a sagging gut, clients
Evaluating them as toys, as luxury articles.

★

So popular imagination got it right:
Somebody hid. There, inside the swan,
Some recondite being must feel annoyance;
Somebody's daughter, having no property
But swanliness, could she ever be sure
Whether she wanted out or might stay in?

★

So much of being, in those days, was hidden.
In various creatures plenitude hid, no doubt
Scant comfort during years of high taxation.

★

Now at the drop of a hat the individual
Burgles the store for significant properties,
Wants nothing to be hidden. All that hides
Has to be rooted out. I do not suppose
The swan's annoyance has to do with that.

★

We mean to fill until it hides again
An emptiness the world we make is full of.
Our keen demarcations hardly swing,
Prolific, round a keynote: time was wise
To be not often on our side. Or else
We might never have failed to suffer ourselves
Enough to empty all the plenitude out.

(From *Die Nacht des ungeborenen Lebens*, 1934)

The Ragged Verses

Secret grievance, what could it signify now
If a writer feeds with it the foul hobgoblin?
The solipsist is limp, self not centred,

Mere peripheral ego, gliding anyhow,
Has perhaps the word. If evidence were untidier,
Might the mind I try to speak be bloodier?

What good can it be to pronounce on things
With no measure for the unsteady
Heartbeat that still drives real happenings?

Horse-whisperer, Mongolian fortune-teller
With your bird bones and aromatic grass,
Spirits, approach, I ask you, also old lamas

With dice to tell for how many more days,
Myself, I may contemplate and praise
Some prettier events that made what's vanished

Valuable now.

⋆

Over a bowl of soup
And with a gulp of wine I recall the cantaloup
A woman in the sunburned alley held to her nose.

Great chords of Mozart sounded in a house,
Then waves of his clarinet; soon Bach
Was mapping Europe with a transverse flute;

There little Miranda crouched, capturing snails
And watching their behaviour in a pail
She'd rustled up from nowhere.

There was the boy outside the Café Pons
Who beat his drum so loud it was a nuisance
In the bedroom where we shook off our clothes

And took to one another. The enormous house,
Empty, in the village, was a vortex
For exploration everywhere around –

Dawn on the mountain's back, blue archetype,
And cool summer air, a hand in yours, and see,
The sun pushes its distant pinprick through a crack

In the skyline.

★

A visit once to the stone
Habitat of a granny who could tell
That Knights of Malta must have gone

From there to Jerusalem,
Or Rhodes, and slivers of shrapnel still
Coiled in the path we took to cross the hill.

★

My book is not drowned yet. Who'd
Ever not air ephemera that freshen forty years?
So fighting, creature, for the beautiful and good,

Keep an eye on ego. Offer a voice
To time never yet redeemed bearing down on you
So furiously day by day, you make your choice,

Richly answer the moment as it streams on through.

A Company of Ghosts

1

The Space of the Mandarin Duck

Apparently in Japan
One century and a half ago
The love-language of France
Was thought to be shocking.

So blatant, so presumptuous, so brutal
Its violation of the atmosphere
Proper to every person.

I covet, they said in Japan,
The space of the mandarin duck,
There, at your side, beside you.

The liminal duck took delight
Breezily as a go-between.
Tender obliquity saw it off.

A space with nothing there,
Dear old duck, even unaccompanied
And far, far away from others,
Still your space I covet.

Come the day when a volley of your quacks
Quells every twittering vandal of speech
And unspeaks the sweet-talker
Whose voice curdles with money and hate.

The Halcyons Flew Out to Sea

The painting of fire had appeared,
   Flames, in the shape of a gate of fire,
And the gate narrow, you could never
   Not be burned if passing through.
Beyond the gate, to be discovered –
   Imagine everything: orchard, pasture,
The classic city, terraced, on some hills,
   A lake so clear you see fishes in it;
The dead are venerated with white tombs;
   For gusto no trenches in the slime,
But taverns and hussies who have merit.

It was only a painting, that alone,
   Only a painting, even if underneath
A line of verse said what it said.
   The series of signs was arcane, beyond
The reach of sense, in a fine script,
   Not to be spoken but for animals,
A horse, a stork, perhaps a blessed spirit.

What of it? There was no gate of fire.
   There was no land of sanity and secrets,
From crests to waters then no wilderness
   Dispersed the feuds, favoured commerce.
Engines of aggression had nothing to kill,
   So calm the town it never could exist.
Yet feeling put its quick into the picture
   And stood the test, not false but fresh
And from the painted scroll flew halcyons, even.
. . . .
They must be making for that island far off.

Homily Creek

Crystal clear at first and deep
There the water
Swirled at a rush over the gravelstones.

Trout in it, stickleback,
Frogs hatch, and very slowly,
Nobody noticing, the gravel rolled.

Clinging to every twist and bend,
Upstream or down it flashes past,
All blue and beak, the kingfisher;

And Kurahara tells how things that hold
Their places, by embodying its time
Do throw a pale light on the human mind.

It was a manner of speaking only;
Poetry throws its pale light away too.
Homily creek, take your time,

I mean to give you my word for that.

Downstream the hearse maiden comes but a spirit,
Feeling into marble, sees to orange and white,
And in the crocus every cell glows with utterance.

A Kinglet

The smallest
of
the dark birds

picks up
speed
visits a rose

four white petals
unshaken
by wings that whizz

for hovering, however
into its beak
unschooled to suck

like a hummingbird
no nectar shot
Oh well what next

the mimicry
the sport of it
the bird in it

the devilry in it

God was a bit
amused
to be a kinglet

The Avocet

Through shallows waded majestically
The long stick legs, and
Indelibly black on white, as black
As Scripture was, it had
Folded the feathers of its wings.

From its long thin probe of a beak across
Its crown and down to its nape travels
Close shaven
A Mohawk in a parabola.

Which part of an aviary alphabet might
The parabola be? Black, too,
The tuft of tail feathers, omega.

White as white can be –
A wing being folded
On the warmth it keeps –
There is the semblance
Of an eyeball mascara might have snugly
Framed in an ebony eggshell.

How deep might then any man's perplexity go
To come up with a feathery vessel
Of streaming life, the innermost remote
Oyster gloss of it, as this foreshadowing
Of speech on a skin. Night with its quill
Does not delete the days.

For the Birthday of John Keats in 1795

*'If a sparrow come before my window I take part
in its existence and pick about the gravel.'*

On the long way to love and understanding
happen to stop halfway up the staircase,
see without scaring them the wild sparrows.

An oblong of Chinese glass with seeds in it,
that's where they flit and fight, dawn or dusk.
Tail-feathers and wings they flaunt and flurry,
so to hold secure a place on a metal perch –
even glutted, beak open and aloft, they perch.

Never in cool consideration do they form a line
or come to believe that seed is really being;
and the dumb brats, the fledgelings,
learn to be dog in the manger pronto.

From upper perches dangle also sporty sparrows.
They do not drop to find seeds further down,
verminous athletes. Why need any bird
with air its element conceptualise,
as we keep doing, up and down?

How marvellously social their uproarious meal,
it braces brain and wing. O horror to live like that
flock of particles, quarreling, finite.
Beat your bright wings on the windowpanes concealing
jars where all the seeds are stored.

2

Whispers of Rumi

Rumi did not have to become one –
a moment only and he could have conceived
of the tangerine as time's godchild.

Rumi might have become a beet
or a turnip, a lemon, come to that,
unless he had a liking for the apricot:

godmother passes mantled
in atmospheres that cleanse even when they sting;
Rumi in their slipstream,
Rumi did not have to become a tangerine.

What else he did not know matters not at all;
now too there are unknowns unknown.

The formless infinite form of the Unseen
only his heart, being limitless, could know
and liken to a mirror, so untarnished,
so pure there had to be a tangerine in it.

The Pendulum Stilled

Homage to Bruno Schulz (1892–1942)

He wrote of a stillness
taking hold of the pendulum

as a condition required
for a creation to be surfacing.

Here and now, fragile goblin
reaching past the back of beyond:

can he out of torment have imagined
words to hold time in suspense? It flows

one way only; only myth
corrugates the surface of mind

perceiving time otherwise – as
a measured starburst, radiant node,

gardens of fathomless light.
Pendulums don't take issue

with gravity but go along with it.
The round copper disc I remember –

hung in a Cromwellian clock
which had an hour hand only –

swung just as it should.
In itself the disc lay still,

its ingredients unmoving:
matter involved in itself –

the clockmaker knew it –
had a stillness all its own

and would not change as fast
as the centuries that swung.

Then he brings into leaf
the packed forest of attics;

beech trees in his windy Poland
raise their arms and scream.

Eternities in constant motion,
that can of worms, tight sealed

and put away as heresy
by the centuries of Christendom –

he opened it, wormless, out poured
the newly beautiful atmospheres,

forms altered, all afresh, on deer
arabesque antlers, auntie a petal

of ash. Tissues of nightmare, spirals
and solids of darkness from heaven

envelop the horsefly, his father
alive in the wallpaper, there,

and the crows like gusts of soot
flock in a twilight streaked with yellow.

Allegorically he lived, to invent for us
a last Cockaigne, with quiet smiling.

Typically for his worst of times
point blank SS-man Günther shot him.

Apropos *The Golden Ass*

There it is
   the albino squirrel
      nibbling rosebuds

So nice a set
   of phonemes you might fancy
      the animal intended

Metamorphosis
   into a second-century
      Afro-Roman novelist

Where do they hide now
   beautiful islands
      Hölderlin put on the map

Here come hordes of inventions
   uprooting the right note
      throwing the goddess a bone

A True Tale of the Anecdotes
Improvised by Villiers de L'Isle-Adam

Ropes in their coils now the men have cast off
And the Mariner eyes the deep –
So in a bar that is gaslit
And homely to him, though it reeks of piss,
Villiers would begin, impromptu, an anecdote.

Marvels he spoke, and the air burned them up.
Marvels, we say, for they were not bookish.
To this day the bright legend travels by voice.

But when invited to collect between covers
Some of his stories, Villiers
Could barely account for those he had published.

As the Mariner puts in at a hospitable island
For supplies of water and meat,
So Villiers knocked on the door of the Master.

Welcomed in, Villiers watches the silent
Master withdraw into a room apart.

Soon the Master is stepping forth with an Album:
Saved from the daily papers and reviews,
All the stories Villiers could not account for.
The Master had harvested every tale in print.

Of the impromptus not a scrap
Came down to us. All went up in smoke –
Gone with the old Parisian reek of piss.

True, their *fraîcheur* had to fascinate as much
As anything Villiers wrote on paper:
And now even more so –

                    As long as the anecdotes,
Richly flowing, leaped toward horizons of hasard,
Make-do phrasing likely
Tempered the thrust of recital; but
As the legend about them prospered, those anecdotes,
Not in the least bookish, lit all the faces up.

Even in ink, unbookish tales
Such as were spoken in gaslight once
Might be no mirage: Eldorados for feeling,
Not even the ghost of a message in them;
Life-giving their book of mysterious vagaries,
Like space the Mariner houses in his compass,
Evolves to measure and in perspective.

For Shuntaro Tanikawa

There's a new poem of yours which begins
'I went back alone to the old days' –
how truly now
your words define where I was going
in my skin of the old pulses.

Modern and strict as that poem is,
I worry that another one
celebrating the flight for joy
of words in a poem
will (since you have authority)
be misinterpreted:
you commend nowhere highflown hokum,
confectionary camouflage.

There may be feathers but the wings
are not of angels.
There must be elasticity in the tendons
or else the wings can't beat;
poems need also iron – not heaviness
but a strong beak – I mean defiance,
a supple, agile
conjugation of metal and magnet.

Pegasus has floated from the stable;
Furies, Harpies, keep your distance.
If poems now are stumbled on,
their ground at least is sure.

No denying it,
your shoes are placed
in universes you awaken, not for plodding
but for a dance. Intimate
observations arrived at while gliding
convey the spirits also
of your translators.
Only for a god and fishes
were winged heels once made.

3

A Saddle for Daedalus

In the saddle, round the edges
Of its fine and agèd hide,
I set, blood-red carnelian,
Turquoise, serpentine,
Some gems in silver casings.

Black, alive, undulant
As the animal I took to heart,
Whose skin I stripped and tanned,
The thing is light and supple;
It has a smell, believe me,
Of belts and wax and ocean.

My model was an island,
Yet the shaping of the saddle
Makes it look as if it moved.
There it trots and speeding up
Sails across the pools and hedges.
So the island started flying.

Daedalus, to make a saddle
I switched the letters of your name;
The anagram was lighter far
Than the labour of a labyrinth.
Harder than either – to decide
Which horse to ride.

Faux-Naif: The Reverie

It was no mistake,
The crystal cave was there.
In the cave, no light;
A crystal coating can't be seen,
But is believed.
Perhaps its mother was,
As at Porthcothan,
Heavy rock and black.

Inside the cave at last.
Often it was fancied:
Inside me here it opens,
All for me, all my own,
Yet no possession, not a cave.
Now, how come, you got inside it.

So to proceed: there, altarwise,
On a table floating in mid-air it rested
Placed by the Unknown –
Of all your loves the Other,
Who might have been.
Call this thing by name
And up in smoke it goes.

Did Columbus never pierce
His boundary of thought,
Of sentiment his bubble,
But goggle at the painted people
Through the only lens he had?
Did they do the same?

Don't reach out, don't touch or
Ever take it off the table.
Consider. Then find it neither
Is nor looks like any bauble
You remember knowing.

All at once your boundaries –
As with one flutter of an eyelid –
You
Or nobody familiar
Contracted them again;

Unwilled, unwanted, comes
A change of register, the crystals
Glitter, floods of freshest
Who knows what
Disclose a goddam flower pot.

A change of one degree
In air-pressure drives you back
And through the cave's mouth out.

So receding, tinier
And tinier, still you find the force
In a thin voice to pipe
Of hot and cold, pure space,
Palm trees, ice floes,
But bliss in a flower pot.

Russia and Holland

Somewhere in Russia a turnip lantern shone;
Discovered there by Robert Byron
It chanced to be emitting music,
Music and aura. Robert
Had magnifying ears and eyes;
Believe you me, his turnip lantern
Did hum, did shine.

                    Elsewhere
Quiet varieties of Russian beet
Left purple liquid in the bowls.

Nights now I miss
Hours of sleep. No turnip lantern
Entertains me, no scent of it
Reassures – the effort
Not to shriek is gruelling.
If I had one, where to put it?

                    From the street
A passing light pulls a spectre up the wall.

Picture with its rooty tones
A turnip then in Holland. Shimmering radish,
Rosy mango, plum nestling on a platter,
Apricot a minim in a tune –
They'll find and warm some walls in Russia.

The Legend of St. Jerome

From Jack Sparrow's breast
a feather
fluttering in the mesh

of an insect screen
looks so little from here –
the writing desk,

a padded chair – you barely
warm to the grey of it, you come
on next to nothingness.

On floorboards the little dog,
shocked by it,
had pointed his ears,

and Jerome at the window looked
the bonfire in the eye,
Jerome

called its figures out,
of human with divine
a dance.

A Tarahumara Jug

Empty, the clay hollow
Has the colour expected,
A dull yellow, dull rose.
When water fills the jug
A far darker shade slowly
Invades the neck, clouding
The comfortable belly.

Changing its hue
The filled jug gives off
A quite exciting smell,
Smell of Etruscan tomb,
Or of a damp tombeau,
Mixes with a light
Savour of hay fresh cut.

A waft of it, at a meal,
Wipes all appetite out;
You join the Tarahumara
Runners but know
Nothing of the urgent
Messages they carry,
Of their language,
Of their footsoles,
Of their lungs.

                    Yet
There you find yourself,
Amazed at who you are,
By a smell to them familiar

Psyche again transported:
Now in their deep valley,

A flock of chickens squawking,
Stand then among the hammocks
They hang inside the huts;
Soon along a trail you pad
Not wondering at the eagle,
And for the rabbit feeling
Not one twinge of compassion.

Also you hear the whirr
Of a potter's wheel, a sound
So ancient, ancient as
That smell of the wet clay,
As the Tarahumara footsoles
Lightly, quickly padding,
As the messages that press
On skin or paper or tongue.

But then it was said
That the shell of a vessel
Has need of its hollow,
That vigilance here,
When the horror strikes,
Must of its dream
Take still greater care.

An Archaic Greek Vase Painting

From left to right the long-legged
Triangular torsoes, wasp-waisted
Figures step in time. On all four chins
Trim pointed beards can be discerned.

Black and white and on each side
Of the procession, small figures,
These too of men, had to be small: their stature
Allows for the curve of the vase
A potter projected his picture on.

★

Do they dance or are they carrying
Stiff on a board, dead but identical,
A male who is prone and turns his back on you?
He looks taller than his carriers.
Possibly they would be ephebes, and him –
Their modern champion, or Achilles.

★

Above the dead man there's a dense,
Ah, but before I get to that
I must mention the conspicuous letter M.
The letter M appears in spaces
Between the dancing carriers and around them,
As if to voice the whole town's moaning.
Some other little shapes are interspersed,
Baby helix, geometrical moth.

★

Now for the dense honeycomb of diagonals
Darkening the oblong above the corpse.
It is earth perhaps. Perhaps underneath
The dancers are not carrying him at all.
They lift their arms for the dancing;

They dance to honour a man entombed.
If he is entombed, the burial custom
Has been for the picture's sake modified,
He's lying not curled up or on his back,
But on his side, so that the harmonies
Of torso, hip, and calf-muscle, such as his,
Alive or dead, could always be admired.

★

Eight tiny women, tiny because
Distanced by the upcurve of the clay,
Quite still they had to sit, above the honeycomb,
All facing to the right; lifted arms,
Palms laid flat on top of the head,
Copy the poise of the dancers underneath.

★

Between the women, white voids enclose,
Just look, with little rays shooting out,
Nine suns or stars, but they could represent
Just as well the seed of flowers in flight.

★

In black and white the scene spoke:
Polarity, a formal drama flesh acts out,
Gladdens or hurts, but harmony is constant.
Women and men, living and dead,
Young and old model to their measure
Moments of night, moments of day;
As for their gods, who do not break faith
Piloting now and then people home at last,
Rites trim their mass but not their beauty.

Significantly less than seven inches tall
This formal scene, a glimpse. Taken off-guard
We know that what we know will not be all.

4

During The Aftermath

1

Some Germans must have had a nicer attitude to death
but in Flensburg was a sloping guillotine
in shape so like the slide
in a playground for the children –
headfirst down a bed of steel you slid
and at the bottom or close to it
the blade, timed perfectly for weight/velocity,
dropped … So like a slide
(with oiled, polished levers at the top
and a technician to calibrate the dials)
you had a little time remaining
to think they killed you not just for now
but for the better part of your lifetime.

2

That covey of brothers, the sergeant pilots
of 16th Fighter Squadron, flew Tempests
and got up to no end of mischief:

one of the dances we went to
was held in the fumigated
military sector of the death camp

Belsen: with their gin they sipped
some ink and quite soon after
gave big smiles to the girls they danced with.

3

December 24, 1945
Petit mal had me shuddering on the floor
of a corridor on the line toward Hamburg,
then at Wesel the train stopped, it was 3 a.m.

Told to disembark we flocked to a breakfast.
Now again I come to be the gaunt overcoated man
groping for old food in a garbage barrel.

That is how it is here, millions who deserve it
itch to live in freezing twilight one day more.
Dim lights were on again when the train finally

rolled squeaking into the terminus. Piss
wherever you please, the police corporal shouted,
but put your bloody caps on straight now.

4

On the Königswinter ferry
A breeze from Aphrodite
lifting the hem of her dress,
war-orphaned Margarete,
her come-hither smile, soon
lips parted, Silesian lilt, our
(come together) silly whispers,
so, busy before conflict,
heavy in histories, merest
tokens in debate, some speech
rockets out of the mire;
and in a prelude ghostly,
allowing its wee bit of body
a brilliance, it lives
on a breath out of nowhere to name.

5

you were too numb to feel outrage
when Sepp your friend the Bavarian
Junkers pilot spoke of Poland as
the destination to arrive at bootlegging
cases of champagne. The sky-children
were too long gone to hear the silver
strings astir in hollow shells.

6

now vistas deepen, disappearing
behind the imaginable – to the nifty
organs of creation, to millions
of mutations in diet,
in soils, in sounds, in smells,
to the adaptations of an eyeball,
a beak, a skull, a lung

indifferent, culprits
in pain and yearning not at all
discovered satisfaction, stole
acutest pleasure
puffing on a cigarette;

if not exchanged, however,
for sprat or potato,
in its time a cigarette, rolled
from butts picked off the street, or shared
with that gracious old Pole who sketched us,
could only taste infected
like the language,
sour as the penitence.

7

Should civility to people be the practice?
Britain had wadded with plenty of sheepswool
the brains of her citizens in uniform:
the foreign past was simply not admissible.
Hide your life, by all means, but draw the line
at wasting it to placate brute power.
Some old sweats had certainly visited
cities in their splendour, waste lands now.
How flimsy they had been, how tawdry
the cheap guignol theatre of greatness;
hats and badges and strutting brigades;
all the folderol scared a supine people
into a funk deeper than ever before;
filth as never before had been their duty.
You could have known all this without feeling it.

8

Now catch a whiff of it,
Braunkohl, and bitter cold it is,
the smoke smells thick and sweet
of frozen Holstein villages,
their giant horses
with haunches the colour of rum,
of welcome
warmth in house and friendship.
Pass down this tunnel
under a mountain of burned bricks,
exchange words with desperadoes,
black marketeers
clutching their sacks
on salvaged pews.

9

was every day so crass, not for a moment
ever mysterious? Had a callus taken hold
to secure the soul for fellow feeling
but extracted from the feelings
some fibres of response? But then

one afternoon at a trot I passed –
not alabaster domes, silver spires, bright
pavilions disposed in avenues – a cabin,
solitary on the airfield perimeter,
a wooden cabin with a wonky porch
where wrinkled tobacco leaves
now seem to hang, no trellis,
no fabric for support, whispering,
not quite fragrant yet,
tenaciously from heaven to the earth.

10

by nineteen forty-seven anno domini
there had to be numerous capers,
their blessings like dandelion parachutes
for all of an instant prettified time,
yes, it was Warrant Officer Blow,
a round man and a wag with his badges,
also Fortune's toy but no fighter pilot,
who trotting back to his billet
from where our drinking was done,
slipped on a frozen puddle
and cavorting on that moonlit ice,
could only rise again to fall,
so taking hold of the ankles of Blow,
laughing and capering we spun him,
blissfully unannoyed, on the double
pivot of bottom and moon.

11

You like her, don't you …
his pretty wife for a pound of butter –
him with his rosy face, too,
young as me, girl-wife winking …

I was not well enough acquainted with the cook
and to this day wonder how their cakes tasted
if that boy found a luckier man to please her.

12

Mnemósunë, dear one, salvage domina,
do not let those fractions
vex or be mistaken

('ripe, in fire dipped,' said the book;
raise the pictures, they darken quickly)

or come closer, shadow
lingering in search of speech,
ready to pierce the poison-bag of trauma;
open to its boundary surely there is a place.

The spirit of evening loosened her hair.
Somebody did still fail to collect his wits.
Significant pattern entering all
behaviour that was old
being by incarnate evil dissipated,
as if on a day's march like any other,
into what pastures bleak did we then go.

Four of the poems in 'During the Aftermath' echo passages in
poems by Keats, Pound, Wordsworth, Hölderlin, and Milton.

5

The Touch of Autumn before Evensong

How can it be that hearing these piano variations
on a melody that tinkled once in the teashops
a listener with feeling to spare has to envisage
a woman who holds to her cheek a powder puff,
she's mantled in a négligée, languidly she hoists
a chuckle from her throat and her bare feet
up on the couch, though properly speaking
it's a chaise longue, quietly now the powder is dispersed
in little clouds as she dabs the puff fore and aft,
but how ordinary it is, this furniture does not glow,
nor is this calm the goal of a great rogue's voyage,
even the door to where she sleeps is yawning, yet
she is the one item in this mezzotint
reaching out with sweet talc and tentacles
into here, into now, so you might wonder who she is,
such an ordinary courtesan, no match for the one
portrayed while measuring his joy by Titian,
such an ordinary courtesan and a woman ordained
never to figure in a tabloid or history book,
exalted in her obviousness still, crashing through
to console the lonely, freshen the dismal,
and to turn up her nose at the monkey-man
with his foul cheroot and tilted top-hat,
and next, astounding on her little balcony
a white cat has arched its back among cannabis plants,
and these must be her white-winged doves,
gracefully they alight on a rail, wag long tails
while a drizzle sets in and a bell begins to toll
from a belfry there, bringing twilight on,
and all set to ask if this is the house for rent
the admiral at the door is lifting his hand to knock.

From a Family Album

On a verge of grass
Faintly two people
Pictured, their epoch
Lost in time, unless
The gentleman's hat
Is a clue to the date.

The verge, and the road
Partially framed by it,
Are diagonal and wide.
That is no English road;
Those folks are going West.

Already they do look
As if they might sink
Into the crusty ground.
So few houses, nobody
Would rush out to help.
Nobody is there to tell them
Who they have come to be.

Actually they stood up,
She dusted off her dress,
He secured his hat,
And while they stepped out
Into the set-up, they
Were artless as the bird
Overhead, but flying fast.

The Enchanted Scrivener

His desk   is his crack
in the highway   of the world.
He lurks   all day
in that nook   and is pleased
with himself   when he hears
squeals and honks   and thundering
trucks. At night   while the public
eye is shut,   he scuttles out,
grabs food   hurries back
to stack   insect wings
in crevices   of mud and grit.
Troglodytic,   cannibalesque,
a mutant mantis,   if ever he fancied
swaggering out   in no attire but
the smartest halo,   traffic might
screech to a halt,   doff its hat,
recognise him for   the monarch
indeed of   all he surveyed.
He'd welcome a ride   out of the crack,
so runs the rumour,   rumour too
that several longings   without any object
carry his atoms   airily up,
dropping him back   as if he were solid.

Into the Clay

All at once I remembered the flood;
snorting down the dry creek beside us

rainwater flushed right off the culvert
compacted earth that served us as a bridge.

To deepen the creek bed and rebuild the bridge
I began to dig sloshy earth and rocks out.

From inches down, two flint implements,
flake-scarred, intact, yellow from the clay,

surfaced on the spade: a turtleback
scraper and a hammer head. Fingers fitted

the form of the scraper, and the hammer,
nicely into a hollow hand I slotted it.

No taste or sound, no smell, only touch
carried me back. There again, chancing it,

alarming animals at hand, on the loose a river
raving through the neighbourhood, I took thought.

When was enmity not all around, day in day out
this hunt for food, the quest of shelter –

when shall we smell horses, not fear silence,
will soon storytellers come and name stars?

Then to stony earth I was holding fast.
Never mind how long the bridge will hold.

The Game of Conkers

Underneath a canopy made of breath for God,
where weeks ago, shaped like lupins,
flambeaux flourished,
you trod on it, the casing, green and spiky.
From it spilled or could be picked, all gloss,
a tawny globe. This chestnut
became your conker. At your fingertips
splendidly visible
it had to mean something.

In its velvet bed of snow the nut, if heavy,
promised conquest. The casing, when it split,
was an opening of lips; it meant the skewer
to be driven down into the nut meat,
and the smell of daffodil rose from the hole,
into which you twisted string,
with a triple reef knot tied at one end of it.

Implacable boys, schooled in civility, extracted
straight from nature a weapon:
take aim, flick your lucky conker shattering –
there from a friend's fist it dangled –
Daddy Goliath, the battle-hardened
old champion conker.

Clouds went sailing by. When the cock-pheasant
screeched it foretold thunder. A cloud
Julius Caesar was portrayed as the frontispiece
of his Gallic Wars. But there overhead
silver frigates drift into battle line;
another day you make out, cruelly,
someone's flushed and bulging mother, or

a galleon with a golden mainsail, or the lonely
cloud that shrinks and writhes like us
at our game of conkers.

★

O cloud world surprisingly begun
long before ourselves, let some sunshine
ripen on their tree the conkers. Now in profile
the Sphinx floats from a sepia photo,
for a little thought pairs thing with thing.

There and then not a cloud reminded us
of a mushroom.

6

A Tulip Tree

Tall as it grew in fifteen years,
For the first time we tell each other
The tulip tree is breaking into flower.

Out of reach from here the yellow
Cups point tentively up (forever
There's not a one of them to touch)

And up, so punning on themselves.
Yes, they say to space, we do appear.
Like one of them, face to his orchestra,

The conductor reaches high a hand,
The flowers flock together in
The hush his fingers throw at heaven.

So impenetrable their silence,
For a heartbeat they repelled
The fog of noise spread thick on earth.

(Hôtel des Grandes Ecoles)

Of Music from a Sunken System

So it will have to be
    on the eve of Apocalypse
as Edmond de Goncourt divined:

dressed in the new
    fashionable colours
vaguely connected with Art,

in their flirtations at dusk
    on roads in England
groups of young men and girls

are constantly interrupted
    by riders of velocipedes
flitting silently past.

For why should ever de Goncourt
    care how freedom is won, how
people defend it? At night in bivouac

the watchful king spoke true,
    hobnobbed with his men,
minding their good, his person princely,

no creature of factions but a court
    of justice. Then mountain echoes,
corn harvested, flock shorn for cash,

for trade, and people came from everywhere
    to self-governance, times changing
to be wasted by disease, old or young,

by fate uniformed as shaft or furnace,
    starvelings at the beltline,
prolific abstraction, empire imperfectible.

The crocus, the primrose, forests of oak,
    ask blinded Lear if he hears the sea –
then lambs hop, again cuckoo calls, on Helm Crag

our seditious Kate sang out and saw,
     come to light in half an apple,
the pip turn into a shark's eye, gliding

javelins. Can they be done without, the sharp,
     dark, tender tones that will drown
in spit and bickering … Goodbye,

de Goncourt. These days an island loses touch
     with its algorithm. Know
by the uncertain signs how ghostly is our theme.

Of Imminence

Of Machu Picchu how should this wren
     trill five times on two notes
          unless he'll be coming, how an idle tongue

define the phrases,
     slabs be laid down,
          houses anchored to them,

unless right soon
     round the corner he'll have come, and
          again the heart of Cabestan,

how will it be cooked for Seremonda, or
     George Herbert have imagined
          'All things are busie,' unless

whistling his large
     quiet reassuring tune, round the corner
          the balloon man will be coming.

The Trojan Philanderer

It was their space we had chanced into;
You'll remember surely how they scared us.
Happy in the dark among the oleanders
We heard the horses trot close. They snorted.
Their hoofbeats hurried around us.

We did not for a moment think
We'd done for the day with love-making.
Perceptive,
The horses came with an inquiry.
If only we could have seen
Their eyes, their faces.

Who then verged on fusion with whom?
For once was it awe you felt?

Who have you been?
The shore swoops up this cliff of granite.
Oenone waits here for your reply.

Mother by the Lake

The little black pod
on the bench beside her
contains apparatus that
transmits messages
round the world in a wink.

She hadn't the time
to brush her hair, but
for the little boy who
speaks to her in melodious
Spanish she unravels his

fishing line (so fine it is
invisible from here) with
thumb and forefinger and
patience that is infinite.

The Desolation

Rubato mazurka, heard again,
Never before so changeful.
Not a soul to be seen on the shore.
Nobody stepped from the train.
Now as before hair flying up wild,
Doubtless at one with a gust of wind,
And copying the corners of her mouth.
So the surge comes on and on,
All astir under the skin.
It could be a ghost of her
Went to her home.
Watch again for the tide;
The tide will soon come in.

7

A Testimony for the Deaf

Bruno Schulz, with his horizontal script,
told of a homing flock of crows

that they were letters from the Turkish alphabet.
Ottomans were flying over Prohobycz,

and happily baffled by their lingo
he felt to heart its foreign beauty,

so made a note of it. This tacit eulogy
in recollection of a Polish girl, who long ago

flew to a throne as empress of the Ottomans,
almost stopped my breathing for a spell.

Bruno's perception of the flock and simply
making, on the spot, a magic metonym of it –

suddenly Turkish finches chattered at
my prison window, raised their yawning beaks

pecking for territory; centuries on,
burning in Smyrna, rooted out everywhere,

Armenian sparrows perished in the pogrom.
Then, cawing across Poland still, the crows,

I heard only the crows recite Fuzuli,
no gunning down, no tumult of expulsion.

213

Promenade

This dog delights, my master feels better
For dutifully walking a delighted dog.

God of dogs, how bountiful, how bouncy!
Spirited smells! My master

Should by his measure know such delights,
Then might his master, surely he has one,

Also enjoy putting an end to dreariness.
Often the plague of it clogs human veins,

Then let no litany of drearinesses
Be here recited, even if, dog that I am,

I poison myself, become the scapegoat.
We are not abject, raw memory of food

And ferocity in the pursuit of it boost us.
Whenever time to stop and wonder is denied us,

To wonder – from time to time he hurries me on –
That earth should also hatch

Us tinkling atmospheric genuine creatures,
Soul of mine, take every chance,

Lift your leg, piss on dreariness.

Juniperus Americanus

From the dead juniper twigs with their prickly stems came
a whiff of incense, and as if from nasal cavities into which it
had burrowed issued a burst of music, familiar but now ripe
with feelings of intense fear and slight pleasure, only to float
away consumed by the general shuddersomely boisterous
groinhungry uproar.

The Leveret

Seriously considered going there with scissors,
Going to the garden of the empty house next door.
Pass by, stranger, roses are for tomorrow.

Behind iron bars the little bush rambles;
Notice these old-fashioned white roses:
They found no hindrance in the bars.

Each is a system of cool curved petals;
In the air all around
A perfume hangs, or no, it circles —

Every rose makes of it a radiant gift.
Of course it is all for procreation.
The rose-fate, absent lover, now,

Yours or mine? Who will not have smelled,
When the hawthorn was in full flower again,
Rotting there the leveret, beside the footpath.

Then pass by, it is the others
Who pick off a street the hand or foot
Of a child who stood there a moment ago.

So it's all very well, the rare fragrance
Of an old rose, but
To be abstracted by it, what then?

Then remember the rose of Fontanelle:
Surely it thought, the philosopher said,
No gardener had ever been known to die?

Body, with your cravings cropped by dread,
Living to discover, still you reach out.
In the kitchen drawer scissors will not snip.

What comes up in a free mind
Centuries decide. Our fable spares no lamb,
And old silent soils with immense force
                    fashion the youngest rose.

The Substance Having Uncertain Signs

Retired to the middle of her web
The spider contemplating spiderhood,
A barrel-organ playing in a side street
Of the big city – embody, do they not,
Firing and drumming deep
But everywhere passengers
In and out of the nervous system,
God's blue shadows?
So while the water-closet washed away Gnostics,
Irregular Kafka insists on brooding,
And ravished by enigma Cleopatra's asp
Regrets the relaxation of her grasp.

8

The Devil's Innocence

While walking I hold my sides and stare behind me.
Erik Satie

A lifetime later
   you want to go back,
omissions were many,
   O my, to repair them.
Befogged by fantasies,
   you failed to imagine,
gazed past calamity,
   winced at
butchery they manufactured,
   the herding of humans,
hangmen mouthing
   falsified languages;
thrilled to the victories
   of resistance, true,
but still took in your stride
   the bomb and the lie, amiably
resolved that only from some
   an old unquibbling
trustfulness, little by little,
   had slipped away.

                *

Procedures hid and
   if revealed they made
for unharmful people
   no sense at all.
Besides, screams or silence
   belonged where they started,
from outside perceived
   atrocity numbs you:

unusual murders,
    the knock on the door;
young heads cut off
    had had right ideas –
so very obvious then
    now strictly they weigh,
still heavier, down on
    the encumbered conscience.

★

A valve is what that is,
    so crimped at the top
that less and less flows
    down into it, heating
or cooling, through to the grotto
    of nerve and nymph.

★

Your innocence was counted on
    to connive at the makings
of one or another squalid
    civil intrigue. The wide world
with its infinite default
    was not getting to you.
Glides from a thicket then
    indifference, coiling and uncoiling,
on its tongue a fruit,
    betrayal, for so (distressed
in Cappadocia, 1947)
    George Seferis drily noted.

★

Hanging out in busy bars,
    look now, they finger
shiny pocket keyboards,
    people scanning images
of earth despoiled

of all its strata. Few
and shallow springs
    trickle in our crevices;
in the deep caves fainter
    and fainter sound the echoes;
captives of the keyboard
    shake their chains and nod:
'In the pancake we'll be maggots.'

                    ★

Entire cities mounted on wheels,
    painted on walls the armies
outspread, all prepared, as in
    the aerial bombardier's perspective,
those old panoramas,
    how pleased with a dream
perhaps nonentities were,
    a dream of power,
the whole caboodle had shrunk,
    yourself become the bigger
for it; as long as they gazed
    could this dream have been
sweet, the flat scenario, sweet
    as the dithyramb
of their dance music?

                    ★

And now bitter, is it?
    So when the keyboard
glitters no more, there is left
    not only indifference,
but grievance, that a promise
    from ghostly data
could not be quickly met.

★

Prospero, is that you, Prospero?
   Then kindly summon
Contrary Spirits, have them speak
   among the young and put
into more than a
   passionate few
the light of heart and acumen
   to flush out
boggy conformity. Multitudes,
   we eat (if at all) at dark
abstractly our indifferent
   meal of the jitters, cooked
by velocity – have your Urchins
   mind our monsters,
purge of dross
   the craving to transcend.

★

Then for my Only-One
   I'll trouble you, short shrift,
as I make offering to her
   of language, conjure up
a dress of stuffs
   finer far than this cotton;
put into silks
   a glow of rose, slash them
front and back
   with implications
lilywhite and damask
   indigo, move, move her
to wear it on her way by,
   even not greeting, in company
with the African
   and Chinese dancers.

9
(For the Crows)

Arp's Arcs

Before the squirrel makes its leap
                to balcony rail
From cedar branch, it will
      have figured out
             co-ordinates to link
Its flight-path with its milligrams of body-weight
And how the branch will spring.

          ★

            At sheer astonishment
Omar stopped. Yet squirrels too
Learn from life.
They'd never quarrel with it for a song.

          ★

            Wonder then
How 'older art still seeks
         everywhere to reclaim
From multitude the first angelic bloom' –
            equipoise,
From one who knew as much,
        travelled all the way,
         tensile as the light,
All the way along its arc.

          ★

To its image in the Ionic column
        don't let the demon blind you:
Nimble with it, animals like Arp's arcs
Take their part in the curvature of space.

*

The spiral turns,
      steadily, with no edges.
         The spiral whisks
Among reflections in the pool an old
Claude Monet painted:
             Tell the eye
To be an oval boat and travel in it –

*

One by one his waterlilies build
Hemispheres   where he touched.
Along his wrist curvature came home.

Household Conversation

How Latin: the island
Far out in the composer's mind.
By Orpheus or by Ovid
Moonlight mothers there

Curling rainbows, where else could
Melody come from? Counterpoint
Thickening texture, then an interim
Arrives, of holy silence.

The island is a fiction.
Nobody inhabits it.
No search engine places it.
Find me bearings for your island.

It might exist, but only
Like God in Meister Eckhart.
Here it is, on a street corner,
A thousand daily feet rounding it,

Shops and parks and people,
All hung up in a boring town;
Coolly from them the composer
Draws the intangible tune.

And schools of sound are regional,
Cotswolds don't roll in the Caucasus.
Then why should it be born, melody
Surging to fullness in a wink?

So can percussive noises
Amplified and squealed
At a collective squirming
Have any root in Naxos, island

Where Dionysus moved the stars
(Measure the drumbeat, spin to flutes),
His seed in the stiff
Thickening stalk of barley surges still?

There's your blood sacrifice: from melody
Tragedy came, to be believed
For five and twenty centuries.
Instead, our gardens grow catastrophe,

Tunes cry the long night out
But no silence from us inwardly,
Who are made and meant
To be listening, listening.

A Newcomer in the Small Port

> ... *Or the lilacs*
> *of men who left their marks*
> *by torchlight* ...
> William Carlos Williams

When the sun was coming up
                    over the headland,
And the first people
                            stood in the streets,
Brushed by sunlight and so narrow
The streets brightened up a bit,
                small fishing boats also did,
And the squat stone lighthouse did – poor devil,
        he had found no way to speak.

But the moment he came back to himself
                        he became curious.
                    What *had* been

History in this place
With its harbour where its boats
                        huddled heaving,
History with painters

                daubing, who knows, in the light
        dance of blessèd spirits;
Then detested German soldiers in the Forties.

History even more so
        for the fisher people
Might have passed without
        serious notice. Once the people
Traded with Greeks, the Ionians, who carried
                    in their big ships women,
To put pep into their colony
        beyond the white rocks toward sunset.
Then everything had shifted.

The scent of the lilac
		was Mrs Woolf again;

Lawrence stopped
	feeling quite unwell;
And out between the port's pincers
	three boats puttered
		making for the fish.

Then he wanted to speak
	but not in the manner of Lawrence
		when so dandily blissful in early light
he found the breath to say Not Yet
		to the offer of *pain grillé*.

Hear him then: Fathom our moods who can,
	how mindfully they hold
		intricate fibres together,
and as the coves of white rock
	contain silence in the water,
		though clay is rammed
between teeth, the great spirits
			spit it out.

Yet when illusion crashed,
	difficulty was not overcome: listen,
before the clay cracked or spirit
	broke the mask wide open,
a devil noted for squalor
shuts the furnace down.

Just Look at the Dancers

Canticles, Fumes, Monostichs

Eleven Canticles

1
Sumac

Sumac knows nothing
of the unhappiness of the past.

Prisoners put to the sword.
Unwelcome populations disappeared.

Over the green leaf you can see
one that is crimson slowly move.

Or should a deep rose be said of it,
cherry, or carmine?

No variety of that bush
ever cared about names for things

or spoke in China to a serious artist.
Human brains no longer choking on abstractions,

customary evils might be repeated less.
With what different histories then

might the finger inscribe every leaf,
as over sand a child carves wonders with a toe.

2

A Difference of Degree

'Three orange patches at the fore-wing tip,
the hind-wing much more rounded …' –

black veins between their fields of orange,
and the composition counsels predators

to pass it up, as poison. Spring and Fall
we waited for the monarchs,

clouds of them came fluttering duly by.
For them the Mexican milkweed flowered on time;

as flocks of them flitted south,
its nectar on the roadside

beefed up a monarch's poisonousness,
and predatory birds held off.

Where thousands flocked, age after age,
now you might see just one or two.

The doctored farms to north and south
made for the migrants an unfavourable fare.

Neighbour, you might have noticed nothing.
Neighbour, by this we are diminished also.

3
Boy with a Long Pale Face

When the ghost of the beginnings
of a smile crossed the lips

of the boy with a long pale face,
what had he seen in your look,

what was he responding to?
But slack-jawed as he was, slumped

paralytic in his wheel chair,
he was not altogether out of it;

so as a curtain is lifted
you almost became really you.

Then will the morning have come,
the morning you notice,

unbelievable, for the first time,
that the crab who walks sideways

copies the hand that is writing;
that all over the air by night,

with two fingers lifting and plunging,
the glow worm types a signal.

4

Sparrows

A Bird of Great Bulk nests in there,
time in his right hand, space in his left.

And he wrings his hands. Halfway up
an average tree would be our ceiling:

for the Great Bulk not so,
he looms over all the houses here,

towering over trees. If ever
we should flit among ships in harbour

and at anchor, Great Bulk would surely
dominate far citadels, deep seas.

Oh but do listen, Great Bulk
will fancy also petty things.

He hangs an oblong from a hook,
full of seeds all meant for us

who aren't supposed to sow or reap
yet we toil and toil at finding food.

By window panes we can't see through
his oblong hangs, and there we peck.

Our swivel eyes detect the moves
Great Bulk makes inside, he yawns,

he stretches, sometimes to display
a rainbow breast, a peacock tail;

and then some sounds, strange and rich,
like music, muffled, come and go.

Hear him crash down the flight of stairs —
all white and gold, he tilts his cap:

when he storms out, we are forewarned,
Great Bulk won't see a soul for dust.

5

The Messengers

What work will build whose brains, come what may?
Who will interrupt and ruin easygoing Indians?

Loud on the paving at first,
Crashing this way up the lane below,

Then between two distant bits
Of masonry, a flat glass roof

And the sharp corner of a window ledge,
Crossing for just a wink the interval,

Soft footsteps and a blue hat passed.
A hush came up, bringing pleasure.

Must it always have been so?
How Jacob came to suppose,

Suppose and magnify and hear his angel,
No-one need hurry to conjecture.

With imaginary wagons you circle your quiet;
Imagine aura, perception returns to it.

6

Editorial for the Snail

God knows they died for their country
but from their regimented place

the big bony gardener in our neighbourhood
who presides over legions of plants

fled sick with fright, the very air
was foul, it clung to you cold, he said.

Time set a handbrake on the disposition
of peoples locked into land, or some.

Bryson has reported that in Oxford (Miss.)
some say 'be' for 'is' the same as it was

in Dorset centuries ago. 'Be,' they still say
twenty minutes from where Faulkner lived,

sipping his whiskey, whose voluble books
lie stacked in the crypt of literature.

Let those same men who violated time
waste what ingenuity they please on Mars.

Past the Pillars of Hercules flit the argosies;
the maps of industry have no room for hubris;

the captains go after matter to get rich on,
no 'diminution of the traces of original sin.'

7

Ichor

At an odd moment in a summer rose garden —
if unfamiliar, it matters not a bit —

even the stoniest of sad old men,
in company with a person

loved long ago and forever lost,
may feel on the eyelids of everything

a trace of the nameless, and so suspended
how it will shiver with healing,

the glance of an ichor that could scintillate
from no lips but those of a Presence.

Where will it have to be, intangible?
Under a younger unthrift sun,

ah, Henry Vaughan, you were there; alone,
not self-accusing, you could hear

a whisper put your mind at ease:
Where I please.

8

O fons Bandusiae

To keep grass growing and oxen fed
thoughtfully cropping it, they pleased

a spring by offering as a gift to it
the blood of a goat mere months old.

So frisky young the goat, he'd sprouted
incipient horns from his forehead;

not even once had the fellow sweated
between the dogday teeth of a summer.

Now the spring cooled vagabond cows,
circulation refreshed by the sacrifice

drenched head and ears for much relief
from the gadflies. A rock hollow

was where the spring gushed from,
and an oak tree brooded over it,

over the chattering freshet
and ripples flowing friskily.

Still take in your arms the little
kicking animal, drink from the spring,

hear the poet shape at his first gasp
with the letter O a circling sign.

9

Early Ionian

Down to the sea we rode our donkeys;
they dawdled in the shallows happily,

and in the sea, naked, for an hour we swam,
then back we rode to trim our orchard vines.

Down to the sea came others
riding spectacular horses;

strange games they played, crisscross
over sand, in surf, in deep water,

men and women. Singing they rode away,
into the blue like gods vanishing.

Some could not forget those strangers;
some chose to go in search of them.

With shears we tend sheep, with clippers
vines, ores from inland hills we haul;

given to labour, for much else we look
to women with all their quirks and surges.

Those horsemen who descended on our shore,
their radiance: On it we constructed

coherent huts, shaped our popular
bronze cauldrons for the sacrifice.

We should not chase after them for love.
It is contradiction that attracts the gods.

10

From the Grotto

Much blood spills in the kill and sharing out.
None smears our cave walls, as yet.

★

To make good I have spat, hoping for a bird
to take shape, a mouthful of manganese.

★

Here and now it will be forever home;
piqued by no phantoms we share and share alike.

★

A sight better than us, the beasts know
what is what. What if we made do with that?

★

We had luck and chose this shell of rock;
river glitters below, with fish we'll harpoon.

★

How temperate now these people are, they think
no gods could come and dare play dice with us.

★

I'll tell a story of how we came to be here.
Pleasure in the design will drive them to believe it.

11
Merlin

For a long time squatting in the same cave
I heard the sea water trickle down, I touched

veins of azure and emerald racing through rock.
What name did they give to that grandee who passed?

Drifts of debris do clutter the shoreline,
empty crates, bits and pieces of children,

draining pus a donkey's beautiful head.
First came the sea for us to step out of,

but before the chaos rushes back again
this red bird will be carolling on a branch

of a young tree come into leaf at last.
The patient sea, how wild in those days:

down the spiral shaft into the cave I came;
at noon I'll hear hoofbeats if the horsemen play,

now and then a new ship crunch into the shore,
red bird sing for its own kind a promised song;

with a knock oars are laid to rest in rowlocks,
stargazers otherwise thankless kneel for once.

Fumes

Not to Rhyme

Our dear homing-pigeon world,
where to settle? When drift? How to persevere?
Why fly around the living in your circles,
evidently unsure of our address?

Catch you, and burn. Distance perhaps
is all for the best. Sufficient for the day
are piles of ash. At the end,
subdue your call, it could torment us.

John Clare to his Muse

If you are extra-terrestrial
Do not stretch too painfully
The woollen sock in which I am the foot.
In the grip of God I ran to kneel
Beside the haystack, glad of the puncture
Of a thorn in my kneecap.
Without limit, what can endeavour mean,
Limit of which little is known before?
Our endurance, not foreseen, surprises us –
Fragile in its body the soul is ignorant
Of being one with it. Without cheating then,
A charm in earth makes cabbage grow.
The uncertainty, he rode it, our Cowper, William,
Macedonian Alexander also. Quickest angels
Speak through a twilight, praise and obey you.
Play me, play me, deafening as the world is,
Hard music for my litanies; never let me
Pray to forget pain, even if they tell me
My memory is birdseed on a windowsill.

What was it they were saying of that Pindar?
A victory sped his memory into the foretime.
Do you come to earth, and soar away again,
In every particular benign?
Send me one day, yes or no, a sign.

In Living Memory

> *'In our efforts to remember,*
> *where are we searching?'*
> Joseph Joubert, 1802

My sacks, my barrow never full
I scout the crash site
I'm not finding the vestiges of man

Such a rare rare phenomenon
A composition of the brain or so
Wordsworth wearisomely droned

Time defecating heaps of change
Came up with sacks of jute and silk
I crammed my cart with some

Sacks full of shanks, a lovely face
Wide-eyed and smiling with surprise
Another with a scowl of lust

I'll stop this and care for the field
Real collectors will see to the pickings
I will return at night and find the field.

The Poem of 2 a.m.

Still he finds home among legumes and beasts
As long as the café is friendly at nightfall.

Still the small voices sing softly shrill
To the ripple's arpeggio on sand at Holywell.

Then time returns, time never everlasting
Remembers to knock on the door;

Unimaginably not disappointing
Charm colours the room with conversation.

Those lost threads find, locomotive again
Among pine trees long since chopped down,

Ceremonial blessing in a run to the pattern
Foreseen, of course, but surprising ever after.

Lozenge, horizontal, diagonal intersect
And into rivers you walk on you will not sink;

Mud swallows the cruel clamour of everything;
Where the wolf choirs flocked what may silence mean.

Nursing a Wound on Blue Heron Island

The sunshine streams
       through open slats
And across the writing pad
       displays a dozen
Bamboo bars of shadow,
       bars of light.

Another day they make
       a stony terrace –
If I could ever climb it now,
       there'd be for me
A path to Shadowy Within,
       or out I'd go
On the town.

Jumping today instead
       another way, the wind
That steals their shadows
       from new leaves I'll hear,
For on the doorstep,
       with wine jars porcelain
And brimming to admire,
       I wait in China then
For Po Chü-i to come.

Verily like this are days
       when the Always-Opposite,
Though virtual,
       disaggregates the real:
On Blue Heron Island
       their pleading we can hear,
Hoopoe and loon and just enough
       the five-score nightingales.

Over Low Thresholds Turning

I was turning the pages of the cave book
when I lit on the wild horse.
Helped by the curve of the rock face,
a white outline loaded with crystal rounded
the body's volume. Hoofs all at once
thudding, the horse ran past.

From shoulder to rump inside the volume
a wavy white line held me from distraction,
held me as it ran uphill and down again.
An unknown puissance rolls through all things,
and with four fingers I was drumming on the table-top
hoofbeats with an undulatory
lull and thrust.

                      ★

                      A Zuni hunter also shaped
his fetish from a pebble, divining in it
the animal heart-line, jasper or jet,
running its ripple from head to tail
of the beast he now soothed
for its life in a medicine bag.

                      ★

Ah, blaze away great grasshoppers and still you croak.
Some few invent signs of an origin and protect
also their containment. Their signs
elude ready measure, often they are
a mere murmur from deep deposits.

The tumulus

mothering the stone cathedral, what can it tell of?
Breath in mind, from its free source, sighing
in waves of yes that break on the shore,
for whole populations herded in barns and ovens
who can speak to scotch the killers' cause
dormant still as a condor's cry in the eggshell?

*

From your parapet on the wavy line
which is a long stone bridge,
watch as you may the stream go and come,
you will not see reflected in it
the bridge's span.

The Lakeshore in Springtime

In long pants and a flimsy
white shift that slid
off her left shoulder she sat
all of fifteen, cross-legged
on a big white cube of limestone.
Side by side with others it made
beside the dawdling duck tribes
a pretty massive wall.

Talking up a storm in an English
mobilised with Spanish emphasis,
cadence and intonation,
her voice young and thin
but bright and never plaintive,
she was telling a Filipino boy

of happy events, party-going,
dancing for Saint Valentine,
fiestas and family things.

A fine shock of jet-black
hair the boy had, and she in him
a good listener. She thought him,
probably, cute, while he
was thinking of the limestone
and of its luck to be so close
to what her long pants hid,
and how he'd build a temple
from all the cubes of limestone
once another fifteen years had gone.

I did not think of Anna Livia
Plurabelle then. Stuffily
but brightening as I now believed
that the conventional similes
have dark roots in truths, all at once
her speech was the brook I thought.

Something for the ducks, after all,
I shut my eyes to see it leap
and trickle, gush and hesitate
flowing wild, clear, and beautiful
from the spring at the mountain top.

I thought I'd never heard
our language pronounced
with such fervor and delicate
vehemence, such
voluptuous undulation.
Might this girl be the forerunner
for an Anglo-Latino revival,
a future tongue for the region?

But I was also wondering if her Romeo
had his plan for a temple ready,
plan to install her there
as a caryatid
unable to open her mouth
for the weight of the architrave
she carried on her head.

Of the Pigeon that Spoke not a Word

While he calls, the pigeon, or
white-winged dove to be specific,
does not open his beak. To pronounce
his call he'll sit and expel it
hunching his shoulders, puffing
his breast out a bit for each
note and its repetition.
Where's a hole for the sound to come out?
Is there proof that the pigeon
hums like us, moans like us,
that the notes consoling us
and suggesting that he is contented,
notes heard in cities before sunrise,
notes that annoy, too, from a windowsill,
have a history to be guessed at?
That bird, biting on the olive twig,
flew back to Noah long before Ararat
received a name, and to this day,
when a need to call surges through him,
he must furbish the ancient sting
of being loyal on a long journey,
of keeping his word across deep waters.
Didn't Noah, even, forget to thank him?
Other birds remember next to nothing.
Other birds know not to twit this pigeon.

On a Poem by Kurahara Shinjiro

Now I rediscover it,
the poem that is Japanese
about yesterday's images;

clouds and the afterglow
of landscape at a distance
are mirrored in the blue

eyes of a mantis perching
on the tip of a blade of grass.
I had vaguely remembered it,

I'd thought it meant that
poetry makes its meanings
atmospherically thus:

You are taken up into the afterglow,
you are right there seeing
reversed what the mantis

could never possibly see.

Tiepolo: Study of a Child

Red chalk on faintly blue paper,
The child tilts its head
A little to its left and is looking
With confidence out, as if to say
Accept me.

The child looks as if only this morning
They'd netted it in the water.
Highlights have to do with this,
A shine on the tip of the nose,
Shedding aura, verve in the features.

Besides, it seems to be wrapped
In a towel or a bedsheet,
Shoulders bare, the head
And shoulders declaring
I am here, accept me now.

It is too young to be talking so
But the lips are fully shaped
And will never be otherwise
For a lifetime. They will be
Pleased by kisses, pleasing with speech.

But the child can never know
How it was to be this:
Not that the best is forgotten,
Only for us, in a matter of minutes,
The artist had shown what it is.

All Over for Falstaff

Barrels of sack
still to go,
night hours
bantering face to face
in taverns
all candle-lit –
always too late,
it was too late
to babble
of the opening,
a circle of them
round a still bare tree,
you could wonder
what was inside it,
the opening, you could
peer deep down inside
the crocus opening.

The Jerbil

Simplicity itself, there I was
          and the harebell came along.
It invited me to share
          its pale I know not what –
its pale intestine.
          What was there was not for jerbils.
Nothing to scuffle for,
          until I ate the tasty light.
In the nick of time I took off
          before the harebell shrank.
Just like this for his food
          young Chingis Khan made do with us.

The Gnats

Surely our lawn will please the monkey-ghost.
Not in this epoch of epochs only
did more and more come to be forgotten.

Our monkey-ghost treads on the lawn nimbly.
Earth grows crusts that crack and clash,
the river carries grannies and good loam away.

Next thing our monkey-ghost dreams in a hammock.
How sweet our moonlight pulls on a velvet glove.
Would that Vega were conspicuous overhead.

Watching for Vega our monkey-ghost thirsts,
she will not forget the lemon-scented beverage,
but whatever she'd forgotten we forgot it.

Oh, I mean how serious our monkey-ghost is to us,
an hour to go and we are temporally revised.
Watch well, never let her run foul of the dark.

Show us the horse that does not shudder
catching a whiff of us. Hear our voice,
one and all, outsnarl the jaguar.

Let us refresh ourself like our monkey-ghost
in depths and varieties of dear life; in the fervour,
the begonia, the badger warren, let us ingest

ichor as yet untasted which toughens its construct,
and always did so while lucidity lasted.
Let our monkey-ghost share with us her lawn.

The Wren's Oration

On telephone wires when the north wind blows
pigeons line up, side by side,
like homodynes in a verse by Virgil.
They warm one another, as after equinox the migrant
swallows make sure they're of a single mind.

As for roosting, Barbellion studied it.
Sparrows in Devon huddled all the night
along a branch. Other birds likewise.
Into their sacks jackdaws plummeted
vertically, singly to roost,
not snuggling up, not wing to wing.

In great variety, small birds quit the roosts
to mob an owl. Owls do not snuggle up.
Small birds do not call them cannibals,
but can't be sure an owl is a bird at all.
Mostly he roosts alone, a hurt bird.

                          He's in the library,
buried in a book, not like us working birds,
and he is wondering.

                          His wife,
at repose in their panelled hollow –
she'll not pass the hours yearning for Rodolphe.

Owl misinterprets myths he reads;
he hopes to see ancient roots renew and reach
into our branches. Forgetting
to be lowly, he sees before him,
while we breakfast in the leafmould,
spirals that by turns bloat and contract,
between egg and ash and egg again,
these intangible passages of ours.

Puzzled
by the zones and their crumpled strata
of fighting, of torment, of food, of the lava,
he expects they have something to hide.

Didn't he know that in its hedge,
when Great Roc and Rare Bird in China
boasted of having bodies huge as the sky,
little wren couldn't stop laughing?

We thought we'd seen, gist after gist,
exploited and perverted, the story
bud and trail away, seen begin
other journeys we do not collide on
and not pettiness or riot but a grand
humility become the condition to attain.

Soil below the leafmould, do not deprave your servant
with scraps of knowledge, dusk, do not devour me,
let me scuffle up the life
with its fine folds in the squirming grub,
with its light that throbs
in caterpillar and spider-egg.

Cypress by the Stairway

In memory of John Herington,
scholar in Ancient Greek

The cypress by the stairway
leading to the portico
puts you in mind of a poem
in the form of a corkscrew.
There'll be a smell to it
of resin, and a shine
glances from a grooved, torqued,
brownish – just what?
but do not lose impetus –
bowsprit, stem of a trellis.

The spiral has to be airy;
aromas crushed by whitecaps
rolled in from afar to the island,
bayleaf and fennel as twigs catch fire.
The handle has to be bronze
from a smithy lizards haunt.
Every corkscrew's body
is exoskeletal, not so this one's.

The corkscrew will be
a cabinet opened by no-one
for centuries or so;
then it is you who discovers it.
A scent of sandalwood comes out,
the brittle manuscript
is in your hands at last.

Petition for a Joint Passport

Flash camera held aloft in both hands,
God stands behind his counter
At the Post Office.

Repeatedly God was coaxing
The uplifted petitioner:
'Open your eyes, open your eyes.'

With a tinkle of gold
The kings ran off up the alley.
The shepherds have no socks to wash.

It's all a bothersome blur,
Or a new-fangled trap.
Let me squeal my heart out.

What you do, I've no idea.
Who's this mother?
Where's that tit?

Café Pamparigousto

Attached to his inordinately long tail,
the mockingbird sings when the light suits him.
He'll sing for nothing without interruption
a song that is perilous and breathtaking
in its alternations of sweetness and violence.

I would like to be now in Arles
when the light suits the stone basin
of a sarcophagus in the Alyscamps.
The hollow could not be more simple,
breathtaking and perilous, welcoming
a tramp for some shuteye perhaps.

At six in the evening I finger the stem
of my glass of pastis on the marble.
Not one thought of the mockingbird bothers me,
let him perch as usual on his present tense,
let him shower with squawks the city of Austin.

I'm busy burrowing into the feel of a moment,
not caring that it is hollow,
into the chill of the marble table-top,
burrowing into the vapid
barely intelligible chatter of this Dutchman
with one ear in a bandage and yellow paint in his fingernails.

One of a loving couple will be alone;
in Arles the shades around me do not dissolve,
and at the street market we find linen bedsheets
from another time. Old market woman,
with a knowing smile you pocketed the money.

The Music Come and Gone

Chewing each and every note,
not in the least Dionysian North
America grew
out of its gold
the mammoth of pop.
It came as a gift,
all of a piece, but never again
could it have come as the concave,
the clear-cut and sharply
self-defining glossy pot or shapely boat.
Out of the air and Greek breath conveyed it
came limbs energetic in marble,
gods in their volumes rippling
and being for ever. So for crafted
instruments a few

fashioned polyphony.
Captured as air from any
flow, any crystal, the voices rose:
Gil, Jobim, Elis in Rio –
Africa scattered dark arcana,
ready the batucada
drummers at the doors of school held still:
Eshu aroused,
people would lose their way to work and dance.
In Spain for Scarlatti came the keyboard,
long long before and northward
volatile Josquin's touch …
A paradigm was changed, they tell me.
Duly then came the film picnics
with Nino Rota, exultation
curved back in, so Allegri heard,
to where it started,
but from the deep a child choir
might call upon the Lord for mercy.
Fictions of deity
made music come true. Young
Monsieur Croche, did you not,
saddened as we became, spoiled
the air we still can breathe,
foretell that it could mingle
with scents from all the flowers,
with movement of the leaves?

Reconocimiento a J.L.B.

He'd thought of his friend who
stood at the corner, there,
of Soler and Serrano,
as a rising saint or angel.
Now he stood in a shaft of twilight,
shrunken face, peevish with wrinkles,
and the friend kept his right hand
tucked into his overcoat,
heartbeat, must he monitor it?
So nearly a saint, and now?
Dear chap, what happened?
Taken aback, he held his hand out.
Observing the disciplines,
always good his doings for others,
such light wings and silver ones
his friend had wished and worked for.
Slowly now, but slowly the friend
was drawing his hand out.
So all the blessed intentions had come
to this. As in a dream he saw it,
the claw of a bird appearing.

Thrones

On earth, in heaven, a choice of Paradises.
Isles of the Blest, Tai Shan, Immortals
tiptoe through the aura and float down,
later to ride back up again, task completed,
on snow-white deer with antlers of spidery jade.

Takt-i-Suleiman, Solyma, Orplid,
Shangri La, sacred cities roughly in mind,
Dioce, Wagadu, or walled and gated
oases, long ago named, where with kit and camel
all will be welcome,
all in safety accommodated.

Best of actual destinations: El Dorado:
his savvy finger pointing past the orchids,
adelante, it's much further on,
not here, said the Indio to the Spaniard,
twenty days, take food, thataway.

An Earthwork: The Devil's Dyke

Only my father had known
of Jack the Ancient Briton,

but my mother among women
knew the anemone pulsatilla.

The earthwork sloping up beside us,
there we walked along, and stories

told that wherever Jack had wandered
anemones grew, for the Dane thrust

a sword into him, or someone else
slain by him had bled to death.

If you find one, father said,
flatten the grass and feel it grow

between your forefinger and thumb.
Sure enough, on every walk

I searched for one or found one,
and soon enough, beginning Greek

I found that anemone meant the wind.
So much blood in the wind, I'd stay young.

Yet the teller of the tales
did not, I think, imagine that,

did not imagine us as Trojans
whipped in war, dispossessed.

That man of music, even Hellenes
left on his map no lyre, no flute.

His Jack the Briton took in his stride
the biting cold, thirst and famine,

made smart implements to answer needs,
one day became householder of

a Roman villa, on the Downs,
unforgetting, uncompromised;

and centuries passing polished
his tale of the weasels and how

a bite or the scent of a windflower
drove them out of their minds.

The Menander Fragment

Soup of wild boar, swallowed by Aeschylus,
seasoned without error, a stew rich and rank,
the taste of it, pooled in memory,
memory of the master reciting to us boys
in a quiet room, cicadas at their chant outside

even among salt and pepper shakers
the wild streak will have its way,
crime dogs expiation,
the animal crawls away to die
and rot in our performance,

to dip my small ladle I hesitated,
in my bowl a splash will do,
the sacrament
was toothsome now, so brief a pang
daylight – everything is there, in the right place.

The Stained-Glass Gyroscope

Hear it hum on a high wire

no immortal song

a long sip from the corolla
and wings flutter above
the flower that is red and true to us

My child choir with one voice
praised dingles where apricot
and olive grew, purples, gold
in our Vaucluse.
Under the ground, nothingness,
yet Iphigenia might be mistaken

Of finest limestone
a sarcophagus hides from us,
and on the panels human figures
opened their mouths
to halloo for the chase

Hear the pivot whisper,
then it broke away
humming in our opinion only
it splinters on the lid

Deep into the earth we listen,
laboured breathing, stone

subsides,
tinkling, the stained-glass.

The Ride from Urga

For something simple, not repeated,
oh, for that token of Attainment –
Mongolian pony going for joy like the wind,
and me on the pony, my conical hat pressed
down to my brows, my thighs in sheepskin
astraddle close to the base of the pony's neck,
my torso bolt upright

and at full tilt we cross immense
valley flats of cindery stones, beacons
and cairns few and far between, the sand
swirls in small dust devils under the hoofs
a long way still from news in my shut mouth,
the secret news I carry so eagerly from Urga,
news I bring to the windy boulevards of Valparaiso.

Monostichs

In memory of Hubert Stanley Middleton
musician
teacher of music
1890–1959

Monostichs 1

Enmeshed in misunderstandings who can carry the torch?

Rugged, cultivated too, some old French people.

Manet's mother's face is large with patience.

Manet's father was gruff, in pain, annoyed.

In Manet's portrait his parents' eyes are downcast.

On Papa's table, a scrap of tapestry, a snuffbox.

Manet crushed his parents into a confining space.

Paint without fear your parents for them to see.

Monostichs 2

This model sits for one painter only.

Once there is a bunch of violets in her bodice.

Again she takes hold of the red fan in her lap.

What a nuisance. High time for her to marry.

Next he paints emptiness between violets and a fan.

Monostichs 3

Village industries still thrive beside the river.

People in light clothes enjoy boating parties.

Dusk falling, accordion music floats up to us.

Dogs romp in long grass, children call.

Singly some gulls slant across green water.

If time allows we walk down there for supper.

Monostichs 4

A knob of goat cheese, fried sprats, the dolmas.

An aubergine in a chilled savory sauce.

Sliced thin, a delicate lamb cutlet.

All occupied, eleven tables on the terrace.

Knives and forks are plied vigorously.

Touched by knife or fork, china might clink.

Carafe here, bottle there, taste anis.

Sky profiles over there the coast of Lesbos.

Wait for it. Supper done, people sing.

Monostichs 5

As an unhatched ostrich Spira appears to us.

Spira is cosily at home in her egg.

Her egg's yolk is snow, its white is apricot.

Listen closely while Spira pecks her egg open.

Out of her egg Spira spills, lucky to live.

Tall ostriches have helped Spira to walk along.

Faster than a camel Spira runs to battle.

Greedier than an ape Spira gobbles bullets.

✳

The selfsame Spira is no other ostrich.

Over the underside of the unconscious Spira doodles.

Of Spira's doodles made, dreams appear to us.

With Spira we deprave complete strangers.

266

Spira runs away laughing with a basket of roses.

Oh, that ostrich calls to us vibrato.

You can't call Spira anything you please.

What an ostrich has joined let no man put asunder.

Monostichs 6: Sequel to Monostichs 5

Past the eleventh hour Spira reappears.

Spira has reappeared as an oyster in Libya.

Much gunfire lacerated Libya sixty years ago.

Closer and closer it is coming, the gunfire.

Spira crouches tighter and tighter in her shell.

The oyster Spira is making a declaration.

The oyster declares imagining to be key.

(Discover good sense buried in the commonplace.

By key Spira means what starts everything up.)

The oyster insists: imagining is the trick.

Oysters assembled on a dish repudiate Spira.

Champagne flutes quiver at the thought of her.

Just listen to the gunfire in our street.

Monostichs 7

On one flank the boats, shops on the other.

The modest promenade can display no crinolines.

Boats at their moorings, awnings to shade café tables.

Footsteps of mortal and animal go pitterpat.

Ear to paving, listen to the click of claws.

A chamois, what's more, Spira has left faint hoofprints.

Wheat is tossed by the wind but singly people settle to work.

Always till noon, from early morning, trestles, a platter.

Why here, Spira, when the mysterium tremendum is your haven?

Black sea-urchins heaped on a platter, shiny spines.

Did not a mariner's eye glisten in the entrails?

Monostichs 8

It fell out that tonight I noticed a hiatus.

Have our narratives retired it fell out?

So it fell out that I took a second look at it.

It fell out that in 1891 Renoir mislaid his walking stick.

It fell out that now I read of this in a letter he wrote.

What the devil, I mislaid mine in a dream last night.

✳

Casual as it might fall out to be this phrase is occult.

Out of what, besides, does it fall?

What is this it that falls out, anyhow?

I infer that the phrase was born from an old bowl.

Out of the mother bowl fell the lots of Fortune.

So ID we say has taken command of events.

ID herds and jostles events into their happening.

Renoir's recovered walking stick lends presence to mine.

Beside this perpetual falling out there are some occasions.

Friends fall out, platoons, nestlings, you name it.

Only the figure of speech tames the raving of Chance.

The figure applies to time twisting and turning.

It affirms a falling out into bottomless Chance.

Monostichs 9

Spira steps testily round the mirror of analogy.

The angle at which a figure tilts exasperates her.

Music is a woman's joy manifest in abundant wavy hair.

A woman's joy in abundant wavy hair is manifest music.

Reversed in the mirror, affectation or banality?

If Spira quotes, where do which words come from?

Woman and joy came from the lips of an Orphic phenomenon.

Cultivated circles heard concerts by the Lamoureux orchestra.

Which of the figures then is the original?

In a moment Spira will shriek at the original's affectation.

Spira trailing a long ponytail suddenly breezes away.

Monostichs 10

As he became older he looked more like a Neapolitan.

Something wrong with his eyes; bladder infections.

Never could they dazzle him, the laundry women.

Seldom could the dancers see where he stood.

*

Golds and greens and reds gainsay his gruff speech.

What of cats? Fellow creatures he must push aside.

Careful now, who else will be a dinner guest?

*

Do not stand behind frisky horses like those of his.

The busy nude is all discretion in her sheen of gold.

Morning noon and night he's peevish from lucidity.

*

Alone, old, almost eyeless he goes trudging by.

There's an even worse war smashing everything to bits.

They strapped to his leg a catheter, an impediment.

He'll keep his stick firmly gripped, he peers and peers.

*

There's a crack in the fence for him to peer through.

Air is foul with coal smoke for him to breathe.

Now there's a pit to peer into where his attic had been.

Monostichs (Spurious)

In Urga has dawned the day to rent a smart new bicycle.

Over huge billowings of earth pedal beside the nomads.

Arriving in the Caucasus the bicyclist is offered an AK 47.

Ippolitov-Ivanov wrote the music for holy space and loneliness.

Treads of charabancs broke the road of jeopardy and spices.

Silk and stories, west and east the lands are robbed of them.

If periwinkles grew there, they died like reefs of coral.

Dromedaries gone, 400 billionaires amassed fortunes.

Rent a bicycle? An heiress would sooner sniff Miss Cassatt's
$$\text{Corbelic Smoke Ball.}$$

A puncture in Mongolia thwarts the lust for competition.

Monostichs 11

The jackals are always there, you can sleep sound.

Our tents are of a textile they can't bite through.

The knell tolls clear from a grandfather clock.

Night air smokes out all thought of biting a windpipe.

Cling to the edge by fingernails the homeless, the heartbroken.

Monostichs 12

Thomas à Kempis epitomised in 1441 *The Book of Job.*

Of old they spoke: Self-will gainsays God's.

The will of God may be the Devil's in disguise.

By cherishing detail drive the Devil out of it.

Worry not too long who forgot her teddybear at the pharmacy.

Monostichs 13

Can a man so bewildered leave any good thing behind?

Redskin left no trace so Evil Spirit could not harass him.

Egyptians took ship for yet another Sensible Place.

For William Blake there might still be hell to pay.

Ingenuity will not delay earthquake or hurricane.

✳

Omar tells a fool his reward is nowhere.

Books ignored, words abused, personal memory wilts.

The gadget does things for and against you.

Now brutish live music deadens a multitude of minds.

*

Monostich, monochord, could you be related?

In the happy hunting ground go seek Pythagoras out.

Monostichs 14

How from a film of skin could eyeballs come to be?

Fish, chicken, man, and kite, a million other eyes.

The manifold of life exhales the exquisite animations.

Rocks and soils are not stabler than submarines.

Give thanks to those who continually find them out.

Spirits of play engage with things invisible.

Nothing would meet us without an impulse from the Imaginary.

Suppose that the beginning was in the Imaginary.

After the beginning the Imaginary struck it out.

Suppose that Spira in the mirror took up the fight.

Give thanks to those who have in heart the Trembling Pivot.

Whose play averts evils of the Imaginary, thank them.

Monostichs (Spurious)

Was not God in the first place a name desperately extended to
reverse the Unforeseen?

Coherences of poetry and painting are victories but still we
soldier on.

Some coherence comes in daily life with effort.

By the conformity of the astronomical universe we are not
consoled.

What avails coherence for the woman whose nose they cut off?

We swarm but are not driven like a swarm of rats.

What avails coherence for generations of the destitute?

Whirled beyond the circuit of the Bear Mrs. Cammel said
                                                    Hello to me.

Now the hate groups proliferate and intelligence plummets.

It is by their proper names that we call the great reasoners.

Monostichs 15

In celebrating the artist do not go overboard.

From Altamira to Caravaggio it was no straight road.

Bewitched by pictures we naturally lost control.

The great picture measures a mystery of flesh and bone.

Seizure of control may hardly at all affect a destiny.

Sweetly on waves of air she flies to the rail, Miss Finch.

Aptly the heron avoids entanglement of his huge wings in
                                                    persnickety twigs.

An image differs: True to itself an image depictures what
was there.

Many many vanishing points for the mountains bordering China.

It takes spirit to perceive right limits for a whole thing.

Monostichs 16

Here's Spira as she walks, unaware of rousing appetites.

The little restaurant has for hostess a young ship's figurehead.

The figurehead jumped ship, she walks among us, Spira.

Her walk is lissom, she's never less than upright.

She does not slope or stoop or sway or plod.

Quick suppleness he also saw, when healed, the blind man in
the Gospel.

See her sail along, hands crossed over her pubis.

Look at the dining space, her motions alter what we see.

Wall and mirror ripple for an instant, ceiling frisks like
impasto in a painting.

To music in a school of dance she learned to walk.

Shove tables aside, make space for Spira dancing.

Algebra, observe, your equations will be solved.

Monostichs 17

Print on the billboard changes, not so the writing on the wall.

With its first white petal cup the shrub rose amazes us.

Return, father. I am here beside the river, fishing.

I cast my line. You turn the pages of *La vita nuova*.

Forty Days in the Calypso Saloon

1

From the Papers of Esteban Seferiades

The Fig Tree

That is where the shepherd stopped,
oriole perches, perhaps a hoopoe.
And beyond is the chasm,
beyond the chasm the mountain.
Still the leaves provide shadow
(as to their shape, the thing is a trident),
orange heat stops
any stir in the dust; and the fruit
falling or picked, it is welcome,
a sight most welcome
in the bowls we set for children.
We did not yet, even then,
decipher the fig tree and its oracle.
From the freezes it recovered,
goats that sheltered
there in the spread of shade,
gave good rolls of cheese, and we sold them
for sixpence in the neighbourhood.
Overhead, too, far as you choose to look,
there is only matter. Intelligible. Porous.
       'And the water-bug casts a flower on stone.'
We turn our backs on it only
to hear the fig tree shake with pleasure
at its entanglement with all that lifts the world.

Ivy and Ocean

The tress of ivy
clings to the roof
aging faster and more often
than the ancient house,
but from the chimney-stack
a blue cloud of woodsmoke rolls
reminding you of a hearth
and of a third way to age:
tame only as their cats
those who discovered it
had learned the hard way
to ask for next to nothing,
so that the souls might one by one set sail.

Orchards in Cappadocia

In the orchards of Cappadocia
there are no land-mines lurking;

at least no land-mines lurk
in the orchards of Cappadocia.

Many multitudes were passing through,
armed civilisations left their marks,

but in the orchards of Cappadocia
the invisible is what appears,

the invisible, inviolable, understand –
you will not find an orchard there;

in Cappadocia no orchards grow
and without them we make do,

or so the Cappadocians hum
round braziers in the nights of winter.

They hymn their orchards thus,
humming high and low and true.

Orchards ought to grow, they hum,
ought to grow in Cappadocia,

because the words belong together,
because old words may flower anew.

The Living Bracelet

Finally that vine, aided year after year
by the earth's turning and the stuff of clouds,
has plodded clean across the window-pane.
It is nice, at an early hour,
to be feeling, as you ascend from a dream,
engulfed by nature, or only half so.
Engulfed, no, after all. Forbid it, as you
forbid the shell exploding through the window,
and civilisation always by others botched.
So much to forbid, you might do better
to ask when the heck that event was, but
now you remember the smell of sealing-wax,
the red baton, see it melt, the match
burn out, hear the hot blob drop. On cool
parchment! It connected then with moss
and cave-dwellings of cenobites in Cappadocia.
Break away, however, from these wings that
open spontaneously and must, must close,
and come, at four, say, to roost on the shadow
projected by the vine over a white wall.
Find there a moving equilibrium. Shadow
extending into the speculative might

correlate with events in nature mere
vagaries that on history have no bearing,
vagaries of a mind its time has starved.
Circling yourself, open every circuit,
in the self-circuit make way for love
of the nearest not-you, the strangest more so,
for there it is, quivering, a maze of points,
reminiscent of the mark, the crimson
cinque-spotted mole beneath Imogen's breast,
and you are whirled into the maze, glide,
glide with it into your cyclotron: mile
after mile of spidery galleries converge
on want, wild spirit, breathless again
in anticipation of an unknown particle.
This tiny insect settling on my cuff belongs
among the marks; it must have, finally,
shrugged its shard off. God knows, long
passages of their lives people clean forget.
Some took a chance, climbed rope
out from between the grinding stones
and attained their arc, waking to perceive
a bare circuit turn into an opening rose.

Rising

These shadows of sparrows
cast on the cloth from Guatemala,
they flit, they hop
in columns of purple bonnets
and ropes of zeroes.
Shadows only; the rebel books,
the hour early.

Let the emperors go hang.
Let the zeroes rise up.

Regime change. Outside
a ruminant state of mind,
and as the day demands,
contrarieties squalling
rush to be announced –

giving a rare whirl
now in the abstract perilous
and on sacred ground
to beards, souks, and minarets.

Returning to Mycenae

There he squats,
        biting his nails,
                our chief;
and I must grip this pole
        or we'll go off-course.

On his way home,
        he'll be nagging himself;
so many troubles with women
        made small
                his image of himself.

Even me, at the rudder now,
        I can smell him out –
        see how he curls his big mouth.
Helen eloping,
        Iphigeneia given to Artemis,
                Briseis he stole from Achilles,
to whom, I do recall, he'd once promised
        who but Iphigeneia.

A man of bronze, lofty
  in his talk, low
    in much of his conduct …

The palace of tiny stone rooms
  in the shadow of the ramparts,
that's where it started –
    domestic smells, but now

now the sea heaves us
  up, down, on the way home. How violet
this coming of a dawn
  we craved; at heart
we were
              not butchers.

The smells drove lusty men
  away, away
    for exploits, adventure,
piracy, and long war.

Nobody really cares about Helen now.
                Clytemnestra,
she had cared only for her baby girl,
whom the chief had to dispatch –

dios, another female, the doe
    shot dead by his archers, to Artemis
        offence, balance lost, unless
our crooked smoke fragrant in her nostrils
        invites the goddess to partake.

Poor old chief, he's
  out of luck
    with the womenfolk.

The stars look right, and not
  because I gaze on them, setting course,
    it's fate,

fate pilots the nightsky, fate
    purges every place
        a delirium infected,
all along with a gurgle we veer
        clear of the slime pit:

        our fighting chief,
he has knotted his fingers; steady breeze,
    I can lash the rudder
and still go speak with him.

A Dolphin

'... *nescio quid horrendum* ...'
          St. Augustine

My teacher warns me: Set on Love the green
mind can only boomerang. Deep then
as thought, your own, may plunge
through vegetation in the soul
to the palace
walled with cobweb and bramble,
and on to the reeking corpse
slumped over the brink of the well,
there's a dolphin, it was ocean,
not an earthly scene at all,
a dolphin leaps on impulse,
and the scales of the dolphin
first brighten, then fade
as the light
of quite another mind
continues its passage. Love is,
if anything, simply a practice.

Theophany in Fener

On the long way to Vodina caddesi
he carries a message, my friend does.
The message will arrive without a word,
and she who receives it will barely understand.

She is alone, her bright hair uncombed
and other street-children play around her.
She stands apart, the strangest feeling stills
in an absent look her delicate features.

Now it is Miriam turning her eyes on us, Miriam
shimmers in the little girl's cotton dress.
She has been startled,
in an agony she is asking: Where do these boys
come from? What am I here to do?

The ferries chug out and in on time.
Faraway the gunboat circles the islands,
and while, nearby, in his palace the Metropolitan
is lifting knife and fork, the witness
knocks twice on the door and is told to wait.

Then to tell of it, no. Deeper than the pull
of orgasm ever was, memory of the face
opened but would not pass his lips.

[Note: Moslems call the Virgin Mary Miriam. Fener is a formerly Greek
district of Istanbul fronting the Golden Horn. Vodina caddesi (pron. Jaddesi)
is a narrow old street on which are situated the Metropolitan's palace and a
(now shuttered) Greek Orthodox church.]

Seferiades

Another time they would ask how he planned
his next impromptu, climbed
the spiral staircase, tobacco smoke
still afloat among the kitchen pots,
the dogs not barking yet in the neighbourhood,
and the noise of traffic low again,
when it occurred to him
without any doubt or folderol
that a poem which, word by word,
holds its ground, telling with no fuss
of the voyages, of the jawbones
barnacled among sunken spars, and tells
of endurance on pilgrimage or exploration,
tells of women wiser for their sorrows,
of tasting rosemary in a wrinkled olive, the poem
made to assail an uttermost
in the rhythms of true love, light,
temperate, driven wickedly (you might say)
by young pulses that suit the occasion,
opens anew the path of mystery,
of mystery that otherwise would flower for no-one
behind the outworks of time.

On the Lakeshore

He thinks those are love-cries from the other room;
then she hurries to the window with its fixed iron blinds.
They rush to the door, they shake it, there's no way out.
They only see, as if it were outside, only as if there,
the white herons picking at the pumpkins,
the soft shrunken pumpkins of another All Souls' Night.
Watchful, high above them, another heron calls;
the call is a warning (there's no way out), but the hawk
plummets, they cannot tell if, on the lakeshore,
it will strike among the herons
                    or scoop the field-mouse up.

Esteban Seferiades Welcomes Longevity

1

The employees had enormous laughing voices,
they cared not a hoot for life and time.

The trembles approximate to their proceedings
no closer than a potter's wheel in Turkestan.

Hiding under green oaks I lived for silence,
only too glad when a banjo perforated it.

I told myself: How should you know any better?
When the music was crass, you made yourself scarce.

If it flies to an accord, against expectation,
again you will sob, because something came true.

2

Words, if I could wreck their heavy sleep ...
The writing is not for writing only.

Of such comfortable rhythms I shake myself
Sometimes free; a mantra must not numb.

There should be action animating an image,
there should be movement, so that, dissolving,

an image relinquishes its ghostly body
for an imprint on the feeling of another.

3

The vocal order of words means to dissolve
themes I propose now and then. In heartbreak

I did not dissolve myself. Never humble enough,
I find in happiness more than I make up.

Peregrine, when I saw your clean swoop
above the canyon, I could not foreknow

I'd see you still, raw, if not quite as then,
driven by the light of origin, this day.

The Saintliest of Men

He was alleged to say that his writings were chaff
considering what he now had seen.

That was not long before he died, aged forty-nine,
and he'd written much and well of how, in Latin,

thought is the form of our habitat, each entity,
(no creature can revert to nothingness)

breaking into a smile from its point in the pickle of being.
Whatever might he have seen (not that he renounced),

what had appeared to him? Before his time,
but even during it, small-town people and villagers

down in the South had adopted heretical views,
or so it had been expediently misapprehended.

For half a century there had been episodic Crusades
to block those Manichees indoors and wipe them out.

It is easy to think that St. Thomas Aquinas
had stood in the Presence, had seen the Throne,

had heard with rapture the old and the young
angels sing with voices to span heaven and earth.

But most of the Manichees were ordinary folks who lived,
thriftily, spirited lives in villages, circling

a domus, where women enjoyed respect, and families
gathered for warmth equitably. So there was a garden

near at hand, for vegetables and fruit they cultivated
cleverly – had Thomas at last dismounted in Languedoc?

What if he saw the ruined cottages, crowded graves,
the small smoke-blackened latrines, where Catholic

troops commanded by bishops and barons had been at work?

2

Confusions 1: The Fable

Originally, so the story-teller began – 'while a bird sang, an insect chirped, and the minutes of the universe passed in their vibrant perpetuity' – originally there was a knot of snakes. Everything was snakily intertwined. The leaves were snakes' fangs, trunks of trees the bodies of climbing pythons, roots (in the wake of immense tornados) were earthy snakes, all writhing, branches were the coils of other snake species, for variation had begun. Heaven and earth were one system of writhing supple slippery and sometimes poisonous bodies. From their eyes sight was given, sound from their rustlings and rattlings and hissing.

Surely the story was a relic of prehistoric life, carried by the Great Memory and relayed through ape instincts, cracking anatomical and chemical crusts until speech conveyed the relic into the vision and narrative of its inheritor. Then the vision introduced a dramatic turn: one snake chose (or was forced by chance) to drop loose from the knot, whereupon it became aware of its independence. Millennia later, a committee of Talmudists in Babylon modernised the vision: Eve, mystified by a Serpent, crafts a story for Adam, so by equivocation becomes an authentically deceptive human being. As they understood it, the committee relished this outcome, for Eve's virtue was life-like, the fruit of a struggle, and as fable it was stimulating: *she acted well when there was danger in doing so.*

The most ancient story, as well as the modernised edition of it, seem to come from closed swarms of people, tribes which preferred their circle to anything as contaminated as a breakaway individual. Cussedly they call upon their all-encircling Maker-God, but as in a mirror image, for he remains alone, as if only the Alone could supply a son whom disagreeable circles crucify, a bird whose breath conducts, through hearts, warmth for organs we cherish, and could endow the snakes with a susceptibility to warmth, which springs into action when one of them strikes in self-defence at the lower limbs of people passing by.

The fingers clenched for writing wait to spread out and join those that left their mark wherever the three trails branched out of Africa, inside the caves, on peestained walls, acrid in the slums of dissolving empires.

Oxford 1949

There were Sunday mornings, early,
and standing in the drizzle
a Salvation soldier blew
his cornet very shrilly.

Almost in the pusta
a zither polishes its notes
and brightness fills the terrace
with quick Hungarian hens.

Desolation of the Sundays, early,
the·flights of stairs,
the holes in the carpet.
There you receive
in grey civilian clothes
the gift of yourself.

Into the pusta, whip in hand,
wildly at sunrise
riding over the horizon
others open theirs.

A Walk from the Orangerie

What a long haul now from the pictures,
longer still without this walking-stick.

By painted willows and the bathers,
baked vessels, lilies, haunting human faces
and a rustic chair transported –

of men and women multitudes –
making new medleys of the senses,
also raising (less said the better)

atmospheres we are wild to fathom, spirit …

Captain and cabin-boy sensed their heartbeat
quickening, and then –
all the settings forth for discovery,
trireme and caravel, pirogue and galleon,
Alexander von Humboldt describing mosquitoes …

All at once at the foot of a staircase
the wolf choir foregathers. Even here
a hood slips over the least exalted state of mind,
the bridge is falling down,
desert consumes suburb and citadel:

In shabbiest silks unaffected the Roma girl
whisked from my toecaps the silver ring she flourished,
and had me believe that a marvel, Monsieur,
helped her to discover it.

Mutual Aid

General St. Leger's poodle, white and curly,
was licking his hand the moment he lay dead.

They dragged the French-bred dog away.
It howled interminably on the porch.

On the third day they found the poodle dead,
but the general himself had now returned

and up there they walked together,
where the hounds of heaven, yes,

the hounds of heaven share alike
in one another's lives.

Even if the poodle's virtues
put collar and leash on self-advancement,

that half the story has been recorded
credits the system Kropotkin described.

O for the century when a dog was mutual,
O what privation for the peevish French.

Elegy: The Calypso Saloon

The saloon will swim in a chiaroscuro,
the waiter will be Gallic but uncontentious,
with a shrug he will agree and pass on by.
The tobacco smoke will be thin and blue,
the curtains of red velvet will conceal
a single door to the separate lavatories.
Table cloths, where provided, will be white,
distinctly polyglot the hum of voices;
of our current passions we will not speak,
but we will not suppress their violence.
Of our errors we prattle more than enough,
we will see how few our convictions are,
we will have polished our sly judgments.
If the company is to be fourfold,
this will be a meeting of some people
who have crossed frontiers to get here.
There will be a future to work for,
work for with all the joy we can muster.
At the Surrealists Goll will thumb his nose,
thunder in August will quench the old lamps,
but the spy at the next table
whom we'll allow to note our tensions
will never refuse us his ear.

The theatre of memory will not be closed
like the hospital window with its curtain
when the wind outside circles chimneystacks

but will not stir and swell the curtain.
It will be approximately mid-morning,
and we will have synchronised our watches
on a day that is biting cold,
or a disturbing Spring day will have dawned,
and the music will not yet have begun;
yesterday's chords still sound in our ears,
Rachmaninoff's Elegiac Trio, the cello part.
Dead in the glass case three letters will lie,
with foreign stamps, heavily franked;
the letters have lain there for months,
but their recipients hardly care now.

How fresh it will be, the brioche,
how quickened the heartbeat
when the doors fly open and Tessa appears.
Walter will be writing a letter to Moscow,
or marvelous things about the new books.
O how they clink, the coffee spoons,
and on their staffs the papers will rustle,
and outside the lime trees in their arcade
will be fragrant yet awhile.

In the Fossil Record

The tenacity of the hen sparrow perching
on a juniper branch hurled across and up –
birds in a body are glad of a gale today –

Bécquer, his quatrains on the tomb effigy
of a beautiful young woman in her best clothes,
the marble hands join to hatch a prayer –

and there beside her a tidy void for *nada*.
The beauty on the slab, or in the tomb
hair and a thighbone, relics of the real,

both, and Bécquer, he made the space for legend
really intense, for this beauty toiled,
toiled and lost, without a Lancelot.

The hen sparrow, blown sideways and aloft,
takes it as it comes, goes along with Rilke:
'Who speaks of winning? To endure is all.'

Some Woodpeckers

Extemporising life
on the flat top of a very tall
telephone pole
perched, or pursuing
in spirals this one the other
up the shaft
fighting or courting,
against the immense
blue but grizzled sky,
with crests of red,
backs that are ladders,
with spirals tracing
invisible volumes,

then a time-out,
claws curled on wires,
keeping their distances,
sometimes one calls,
sometimes the other,
a trill, a contralto chuckle,
beak shaping breath
as a tiny pointed wizard's hat,
contradicting one another,
sharp outlines, slim bodies,
so perceived through a lens
the hour before dusk
and the commute begin –

vertigo,
not for them, their time
spins a small
glittering web,
and not for anyone
anxious to be feeling
the torrent pass and pass.

Take it from them:
there it is how it is,
no sweat, no bloodshed,
observing the territories,
nothing sensational
it wears no decorations,
and is the moment
not yet forgotten.

The Ghosting of Paul Celan

In shadow from the past
I have tried to tell
of what the breath-crystal
in a word rejects:
greed of the eyes to see again,
greed of the fingers, all five.

Against the odds an image,
against the flow,
no pronouncements,
advancing –
                              Thicket, the image
lunges through the thicket
out there, in the head.

Firebomb and
martyrdom, how
neighbourly in sound, by wires
people move, Punch
and Black-Eyes. Wires twist
round cortex and ankle.

Slow image, painful, breathless:
in ordinary civvies
four or five of them,
seen from behind, four or five
dispersed, walk forward beneath
the living branches.

In the red gaze of wine
in its house of glass
there'll be sometimes a dragon,
sometimes a reminder
that trust is for the free,
the foolish, the very rare free.

Sliding through cropped grass
boots and shoes

and then the foreknown
about to happen, any moment
some unspeakable thing.

See then ways they mix
into the mutations. If we cringe;
the god will spit on us;
apprehend the tact while pipe and string
carry us away,
and in the music we are lost.

Confusions 2: The Phantasm

Even before lunch a necromancer enables a Count at the court
of the Emperor Frederick to become lord of the city he first
besieges, spouse of a lady, father of sons, of whom the oldest has
reached forty years of age.

So far the story runs in its early Italian version. Turkish and
Spanish versions are also as old as the hills.

Returning to Frederick's court, now at the age of eighty, and
supposing that the empire will meanwhile have changed its
rulers several times, the Count finds the Emperor still washing
his hands in preparation for the lunch attended by the necro-
mancer.

So the Count had been enchanted, living a dream.

Is there not in this tale the embryo of a neurosurgical critique
of self-deception? Still we believe that our opinions (namely,
our words) about the world, and about one another, are true.
A hiding of the agenda is done by the searchers of what hides,
and done no less by the agents, who do not search.

The tale is set, fittingly, in a political theatre.

When the safety valve of the visible has burst, pageants
devised to distract or to stupefy a nation hide from sight millions

of families wasted by poverty, their masses extending beyond the horizon.

A little agony of self-knowledge cleared up the Count's confusion.

Be that as it may, when liberty shrank to the right of anyone not to harm anyone else, there was a stampede of incorrect, novel, and efficient ideas escaping down the hospital corridors. Before now, its history shaped and reshaped a culture in conformity to degrees of divergence between the necromantic spell of banking interests and the Count's recognition of a washing of hands.

Perhaps the secret agenda of matter is to deny the Count's existence, to become entirely neural. Without misgivings, some of the older poets, meditating on Apollo, took the liberty of imagining their Mother to be a harp, an immense harp.

Such a devotion to Nature was Pythagoras but no delusion. Their secret agenda, to which the Emperor Frederick himself had attended, was to voice the ancient, not by brutish repetition, but by working the scale of a precise and elusive brightness: Rose Window, Duomo Cupola, Sestina. And that, while it ascends toward the angelic, lives close to the bone.

Embers, Not Entirely
in the Manner of Jean Follain

1

Light from the electric
lantern suspended
over the plastic zinc
and in a bottle's shoulders
sharply reflected
makes the eyes of a wolf
glitter from the forest.
A sip of his aperitif
and the man, fascinated,

has for seven seconds
woodsmoke in his nostrils
where he wants to be.

2

They put the ladder on a slant,
the top of it attains the roof.
Then (thinks the man) they winch,
using a pulley with a lever,
a box aloft.
As yet so new, a small machine
still is quiescent in the box.
Switch it eventually on,
its breath will be so cool
that it subdues the sun.
Just imagine it: all night
with no clothes on, no fan
to rake sweat from the skin.

3

Hooded with indigo the head,
all down the dorsum
emerald and iridescent,
its slender claws took hold
of a railing and dispersed
vulgar sparrow, silly finch.
The feathering of the breast
a red so opulent
all the brown birds took off.
Then the man saw its streaming,
its princely silhouette,
again in the juniper tree
with nonchalance enthroned.
It was passing by, the beast,
so the man could then exult.

4

All too much has been
discovered, thinks the man.
This I discover likewise.
Give me the crypt every time,
seclusion, out of this world,
of flesh, of devil, my moods
ought never to be known.
The man thinks: All in vain,
all the seals are broken now,
remotest lakes are drained,
footsore through our forest
we trample, hacking.

5

Growing old, the man dreamed
of death, or so he said.
Death held a huge pewter dish
heaped with assorted foods:
This is my middle, eat,
said Death, eat all of it,
it is the information.
The man ate not a scrap
and understood his dream.
Death, get along with you,
he said, I'll die (your dish,
who cooked the sauces for it?)
sooner of *ders*, a Turkish word.
Let me remind you, it means study,
study that brings understanding.

6

For no profit I intended
to make a paradis terrestre.
Driven by curiosity, by love,
I cobbled some pieces together,
but over the shadow of self
I could not arrange to jump.
Selfish, I gave pleasure,
innocently self benefitted
from hardships borne by others,
small consumers, hostage to usury.
These thoughts the man weighed
while earth-plates buckled underfoot,

swallowtail vanished, roach persisted,
on stinking shores the hardy
scavengers heaped cakes of oil.
Rich self, scope of action, self
like an empire must expand.
Others have their turn tomorrow,
see now the winged ships coming in.
Among moles, weasels and the lizards
the world's end is often mentioned.

A Worm's Theorem

Straight as a bird migrating an arrow flew,
straight as a bird, to strike the bull's-eye.

A second time an arrow flew and struck;
only a third shot will smash the world, they said.

Now comes a pause, time enough to raise a worm-cast;
before another arrow flew, there came a pause.

Straight as a bird the arrow flew to the bull,
and if there is a logic to earthly events,

if there is a logic at all, it is a logic
not of culmination but of variety repeated.

Repetition provides that no shot can be third;
the second shot repeats but is not the first,

and a third shot figures only as the first again.
Variety repeated has to be the form of progression,

accordingly progression cannot culminate,
and varied repetition delays indefinitely the world's end.

I saw from a bridge the arrow fly through darkness;
friction with darkness made the arrow shine.

Triple Hiatus

Inexplicable, these
two young Oriental doctors of medicine
at the bar with its black tombstone top,
their chat of all the recent (seemingly
continuous) parties, all the songs, who was who,
and their alternating companionships
as girl and boy.

Inexplicable the hiatus in Homer:
the priest's two daughters (dark or fair?),
their capture from a few leagues down the coast
making the war take the shape it did,
and their unavailability, being never introduced
as persons who act and speak for themselves.

Inexplicable, why the quality
of the choirboy's voice, singing in Latin,
though the boy knew less about Latin
than about chocolate mousse and soda pop,
resembles, touching the heart, a certain
absolute, pure, invisible
source of a pressure, harboured in nature,
that ushers consciousness into being,
that makes thought about thinking also possible,
and how the enunciation should be so perfect
that she herself who is invoked did not step
note by note through the strings of the harp,
nor did her blue cloak brush against them slightly.

Leonardo da Vinci's Cecilia Gallerani

It is as if she wore a mask
and the black ribbon crossing her brow
secures it once she claps it on.
Yet the mask wears an expression
not of wonder but of a shrewd
curiosity as to what is there
to her left.
           That is where the light
bathes a shoulder and brings out
the delicacy, almost it is Japanese,
of all the features, together
with the small puckered snout
of an ermine.
           Now you see,
as the light expands, this fullness
of the ermine's belly and the four pointing
fingers that have sprung from the dark
to caress the animal spine.

The ermine's head, portrayed on a tilt,
is not attractive at all, but,
well, it is real and not a mask.
You see then that the mask
is all aglow with intelligence,
intrinsically so, not at all
for a contrast with the animal's
beady eyes, pink and puckered snout.

Is that lacy headgear called a snood?
A strap rolls out of it and round
the lady's throat, vanishing beneath
her rounded chin, on which the same light
fastens itself.

                    Bald as the mask is,
all shaven as its flesh looks,
the lady's eyes rest confidently
on something not far off on her left,
something that could be nothing
others would find significant at all.

Whenever it was that the painter
agreed to the commission, within the hour
he was acquainting himself
thoroughly with the physique
of ermines. For all he knew
of women and their costumes,
the surprise by which he painted
this level gaze, its immobility
and all that's woman in it,
all surfaces, the likes of us,
we find it
deeply surprising still.

From the Distant Place

In Mado Michio's poem 'A Distant Place'
the syllables tell
of mosquitoes adrift in a draft
and caught in the web of a spider.
Then we mistake them for stars.

As I remember it, Psyche
was borne by the wind from a crag
into the palace of Eros.
Wedded to him, but forbidden
ever to see him, Psyche lying awake
lit an oil lamp and the light of it
fluttered over his marvelous body –
naked, winged –

then a hot drop of the oil woke him,
and Psyche was banished,
for the divine could not endure the human.

Eros is not manifest
in this distant place, where all is finite;
distant place, where chalk is cheese.

Psyche demanded distinctions. Psyche
seized by the love-police,
suffered punitive ordeals.

Slowly she moved from the distant place
distinguishing this from that. The individual
grains of wheat in a mass of it she counted;
out of the mass she teased the individual thing.

Eros flew back and his mother conceded
that Psyche, in all the distant places,
threw to the wind
every distraction, empty temptations.
The old story told that the goddess

knew that Psyche was in, a deep one,
admissible to the games of the gods,
versed in the rules of being not seen.

It is disputed which of the gods understood
the doings of Psyche. Eros himself
took on a body only when sleeping. Is this,
I mean, what Chekhov wondered of love –
was it a vestige of something once immense,
or was it a particle for us to develop
till it becomes immense: 'These days
it gives much less than one expects.'

3

A Winter Landscape, 1646

for M.J.M.M.

1

All day the same cloud cover
never lifting up, all day
the tubby farm woman trudges
speechless toward the two herders
whom a streak of sun hits. And
diagonally opposite intrude
a pair of feet in pointed boots,
the man invisible, with his boots
sharp-toed, creased like a cowboy's.
While day is dark like this,
winter means cold feet
in the prominent pointed boots,
unless these are not boots
but a species of cowhide stockings.
Don't forget the warm dog in midpicture
plodding behind the big woman.
Don't ever forget that winter
which brought doom to many Dutch.
Amazingly ice prolonged itself;
cart axle froze, the unwashed skin
split and burst, and Rembrandt
trotted back home as quick as he could.

2

Then look again, at the two
fleeces of cirrus. The woman's apron
traps, for half a shake, sunlight,
the herders too have golden shoulders,

farm buildings behind them –
shelter they have quit, this is
a new day, and here outside,
almost warm, we can stretch out,
enjoy a first tingle of April.
The woman has baked a pie,
the men are back from the meadow,
the dog can poop as he pleases.

Ah, they all exclaim, feel
the promise, now the year does turn,
give thanks, the dead rest, all
who did not die stand on both feet,
praise Him who brought us through alive.

3

It is not as you and I see it now;
to each of us a fiddled minuet
or any specific and imaginable sound
recalls another epoch otherwise.
Times are different in character, history
with jumbled families of signs
is breaking out all over.

Likewise in other Russias,
other Egypts, Sumerias, Hong Kongs,
people could for their moment
stop work and cry aloud:
If we were somewhere else, consider,
life might be different in it;
our science has not fathomed doubt.

Today instead we say:
There was a worm making grass grow
up and up. Then the worm-casts
rose with a lawn around them; then
they toppled as they dried, with us

thoughtful inside them as our habitat.
Henceforth we grovel to deflect the glance,

for us the peacock's tail unfolds
to focus elsewhere all its eyes.
What Rembrandt saw evaporated
with many massacres, in temporal dark
and mud. These figures, touching
when, all at once, the eyes, they opened,
with sacred seeing Rembrandt set them free.

A True Tale from Schwabing

There at eye-level before him
Rilke sauntering in the English Garden
while World War One was in full swing
saw a cup with a broken handle,
a cup anomalously perched
on the back of somebody's hand.

A blue sediment in the hollow,
that was Death, he knew at once;
and round the rim in Gothic letters
'HOFF-NUNG,' the inscription ran –
a trace, perhaps, of the old-time breakfast.

That same night, at his lectern,
a frenzy split apart his musing,
which made Rilke, soul and all,
practically modern. Who, he asked,
who can these beings be who need poison
to frighten them away? The hard present,
they let it be taken out like a dental plate,
so the chins are left to wag and wag.

Then he glanced out of the window
involuntarily recalling
that from a bridge, and long ago,
he'd seen inside a shower of falling
stars. Now did he
cry out to them, or murmur:
I must not forget you. Stay!

Fennel

The fennel plant could be rastafarian,
except that its feathery green pennons
are not coiled around its bulb, and anyway
they are not in the least like holy hair.
They resemble, sooner, a memory of the jungle,
a jungle of ferns; sooner still
the rarest of ferns in a hot-house. They sprout,
to be accurate, from the core of the white bulb.
Skins layered like those of an onion, this bulb,
if or when its feathery jungle ferns
have been shorn away, begins at once
to push into the light a new sprout,
and the sprout is impudently erect. So the bulb,
vigorous, with its aroma of aniseed,
resembles the eyeball of an angel. Now down to earth
the bleeding back of it has turned
on us; now the ferns are playing,
in a manner infinitely remote, their angel eye-beams
across a heaven emptied of God. So then –
how come this morning for an instant
the fennel did look lifelike?

Of the Mistaken Mendicant

Slowly some evenings
pass. At least
he rises to it, giving in
to solitude,
making its return, though welcome,
freeze stiff
the forest of his mind.

As dusk
also returns,
with all the excursions
to places, the exchange
of words with people,
whole-hearted, and,
threadneedle-fingered, the
two dark women
in particular, since
the third has not yet come,
death does not.

Daily the hunter constructs
the blind he is in.
What is this, such
a thirst for the dust
of a journey,
short, to candles
on the bar counter,
or long, to the lakes
neighbouring great

foreign libraries,
the coasts and the boats,
a smell of cutlets grilling.

And tonight, tonight
he was there, there
to tell you only

that time, persuading you
to imagine nullity,
from heavens and hells
flesh could not endure,
also protects you,
the inhabited past
and desert future
being all atmosphere.

The Spring Sunday

In the western sky, flattened by pitch dark,
a couple of planets
brace for conjunction.

At the laundromat door –
a speck of mascara dotting each
faintly pink eye-pocket –
my neighbour is glad they are beautiful,
there up the stairs in the pot,
those white roses of mine.

Dogwood lit its candles, some trees green all over,
the shoulders of some roads are lupin blue.

She's washing some sheets,
she has swept the floors, now her daddy,
so she whispers,
wants to go out, go out to play.

For the unknown wife
red bird calls I am counting
twenty-six distinct
clarinet notes on bated breath.

Stooped and tottering daddy, his jaw
set for a groan. She who shrugs,
who gives him her space-time –
inside vexed features perceive the hero
making a place fresh, claiming her day.

A Hatful of Spectres

A Dresden Teacup
A dell, a pit, the ghost
of willow pattern in it,
then the barbed wire in it;
blue streaking white now,
the barb is a hurricane lamp
hung from an arch in a *Laube*;
this arch being theoretical,
aptly bulbous flowers cling
to columns that are spindly;
a flower clock in the saucer,
still the barbed wire snags.

Epicure
Look, as into a well,
down in it, deep,
and not too far off
white roses, seven, lift
from earth in their pot,
and chimes
carried here by the wind
from another porch
caution: take heart,
feel only for today.

The Staircase
Of all places, here,
propped between
assorted pens and me,
an old stone staircase
in an old foreign neighbourhood
rises between some trees
to a lamp whose lunar glow
is like a silver fruit.
Windowed buildings, just a few,
flank the stair;
deserted by their foreigners
they now preserve the silence,
a mother to my ceremonies.

The Ash Tray
with a gilded china handle,
taffeta curtains round the rim,
and on its bottom an anemone
painted with exceptional skill –
but it was stolen from an elf
who sat on it to defecate,
and an elfin maid would take it
by the handle, empty it, and lo,
reveal the flower born of wind.

Morsel
Morsel begins in Sanskrit.
Carried into Latin
still it signifies a bite:
mouth not even full,
but a pictured thinking
made of it remorse –
the bite in the back,
regret (falling short of penitence),
a hurt come home to hurt.

From a party dish
many fingers take the morsels.

Blue shark remorse
haunts the sea of money seldom.

Chairs
Some chairs sit
like people
with arms
outstretched
for balance
in the absence
of a head.

Ah, how ardently
the chairs do beg
to be sat on,
arm in arm,
back to front.

A Bronze from Kerala
It does not have to be a god.
Tapering headdress towers up and all
is motion in the arms, the face
small and against the light
featureless, yet by the bronze
fashioned to weigh perhaps an ounce;
and stiff in the bronze
he'll do his dance, destroying us;
his flame is busy, eating time,
so a rigorous semblance here
gesticulates on a box for now,
one with the unrelenting
responsion of the tides.

Neolithic
Like skin during massive surgery
earth by a blade had been folded back,
another forest floor looked at the air;
he wandered across the work-site
and of a creaking tree he asked

(thirteen years old and fancy-free)
what harm might they have done to it?
Pretending to be him, the tree replies:
As a reward for sympathy, you
may make a wish. At once he wishes
to find an arrow-head and place it
beside the scrapers in his collection,
and from the earth newly exposed
he picked one up, 'willow-leaf,' honey-blue,
the arrow-head whose flaked surfaces
still answer to his touch.

The Bedevilment
It is a far cry to the object, and the cry
to a purely imaginary object is silent.
Absently, if at all, the imaginary appears
while a real thing is being invented.
In the twilight of a room of my own today
two books lay flat on the floor; I looked,
and the thicker and smaller book lay flat
and flush on the other. Make no mistake,
what I saw was a picture, the frame double –
an inner frame juts up, its higher edges
contain (never noticed before) this picture
of the backs of old books I'd always looked for.
They line up in the picture, on their spines
are tiny old labels with names and titles;
the bindings are of a pale blue or grey,
stitched in the early 1800s, and intact.
An enduring imaginary object seldom finds
its way into the world, like peace itself.
Whatever is called into question
by an extraction of shadow from real objects,
whatever they die for in Homs, in Cairo now,
still I would find a fugaw or boyne agreeable,
a spargon, a megaluz, a string quilp.

A Pine Siskin

The bird is not aware of its markings –
stripes that cup the spine are definite
and arched like the ribs of a cathedral;
the leading edge of its wings was yellowish
and finally gave it away.

We knew it and it was pecking
untroubled by our presence
on its patio, pecking in the cracks
between some broken paving stones.
It fed on grains too small for us to see.

An entity secured
by markings it was not aware of –
it blended in, wherever it flew,
or so we might suspect,
into every order of wood and plant it blended

easily, foraging at a distance
from its home in a conifer,
or home was also here, among flowerpots
and the interstitial cracks
kept the creature deeply occupied
with a part it played, there, in the drama.

It stayed there, so remarkably pecking
close to the table, close to our dishes,
that the stranger in our midst
told of a blue robe,
of a virgin clothed in it,
of the creature in its folds.

Then for the few moments as we watch
we have forgotten our mortality,
the deep itself. We might shrink; being
absorbed by it, we absorb
the siskin's grace. The spunk of it,

the trust — we are silenced,
or we make fools of ourselves.

The conifer's remotest ancestor
and what opened organs,
squirming, serpentine, godlike,
to rid itself of a primal egg,
blithely the siskin
on a hairline of convergence
and idly we ignore.

The transformations puzzle us;
turbulent mutation, huge and slow,
baffles our interest, always
elsewhere, so displaced
we mean to fix things as they are,
we ask the company to stay.

Water at Not More than Six Feet

*[Where] we find these drawings, we find
water at not more than six feet.*
                    Leo Frobenius

It might be that I did what I had to,
that the turn I took was a random swerve
in the nick of time, otherwise
I might not have done what I did.
The great grey blur lurks
at the start of where chance moves into choice,
and is still astir in our acts,
and the consequences
at the time unknown are later
entirely forgotten. It seems
that the flash of intelligence
and dexterity that gave

a Hittite to turn a lump of rosy clay
into an elegant jug, a jug
with an embonpoint like a baby's
and a broad loop for a handle –
what was it now that seems
the thing I'd been going to say?

And the fathoming of matter
was not done by transient solo
makers of models and of equations
that drop off the end of the blackboard.
It was done by successive generations
who acquired, piece by piece,
a knowledge and made of its vestiges
models more likely to match
a huge dark cavern where the neutrino lives.

So it takes attention to a savage music
phrasing memory for me to hurdle
my blind actions and their consequences.
Or that is not so, quite likely we hurdle,
to attain the drawings and soon the water,
a gate that the angel could float over,
a gate that otherwise encloses
into mechanisms of its own
our diminutive pocket of plasm and muscle
which dispenses the thimble of daylight it is greedy for,
but calls out the roosters at their first blink.

A sometime never to come:
It is not given me to go
into the tortuous tubing of dismal souls.
In mania and mixed-up ideas
I have found nothing I looked for.
So I rend myself apart
and the days of change, of smiling again
seem to be over; of millions beyond help
sing, dodo, lightly the blind words will pass.

Confusions 3: The Belief

No, I do not have time to look it out, a poem in prose by René Char; it has to do with a painting by Latour, in which the glow of an oil lamp casts a light on the face of Magdalene.

Why another glowing light leads to this impetus in writing I cannot tell. But a connection produced a gentle shock.

Wearing a turquoise and frilled dress, waiting for her friend to reappear at the bar, a young woman held up a cell-phone and received, all around her eyes, above the cheekbones and below the hairline, an oval of faint light.

In the glow she was looking into a microscopic encyclopaedia, so I decided. Fair hair combed back was caught up in a ponytail. The dress contained, for the duration of the glance that noted the V-neck, a voluptuous body in the twilight of the bar.

Solitary for the moment, absorbed in her encyclopaedia and masked with an oval glow in which one eye glittered, she held me spellbound. Her friend came back in his flat cap, it was no concern of mine, but I could recapture, there and then, Latour's picture, and now I understood the lunar allure it had for René Char.

The little event had some importance for me, but none for the young woman, who is already, while I write, forgetting all about it. A capacity for belief, hallmark of the species, lies behind the formation of empires, behind prejudice such as authorised any number of martyrdoms, behind any number of vile or heroic acts, it is the engine of discovery, of love, and of the arts, but now and here it was a mere assurance that Another has drawn attention, has glowed in the light, and may again, always again, be there.

Had Constantine misread an X, he could have come to grief. After rounding the traffic island, you may doubt which side of the road you are on. The gentle shock had not come from a collision, but from a brush with an entirely altered outlook.

With a thrust from belief, even while I observe images that flash across the interior walls, I break out of my shell. Magnified, the process may seem (as it did to Tertullian) absurd. At least for as long as I was looking, Another was there, alteration occurred, an oval of aura in the locus of the sacred was a sign to follow.

Being an effect of distance, belief also has a penumbra. Out
of the penumbra crawl fraud and superstition. Of what does the
bubbly German word *Aberglaube* give a hint, if not of the pande-
monium deposited by belief behind its own back. There, if
anywhere, Another is evil. Magdalene could not be identified.
A dupe on the road to paradise blew her to pieces.

On Setting Out by Stagecoach
for the Southwestern Territories

A Japanese travelling alarm-clock
ticks away the seconds of the universe,
and the pulse in this wrist of mine,
though I hear and touch,
steadily still refuses to be synchronised.

Immense silence swallows our inmost
moral tip of the nature of things;
the silence, barely perceptible, weighs
on our languages that are born of harmony
utterly incorporeal, powerless
to take a mystery up on a hook.
Poetry pure but prim –
a tomcat up high in a tree calls for help
to find the right way down.

If then a tongue can accommodate gibberish,
let it laugh at words presumed official;
discover surprise, beauty's contrariness;
admit some sense at least from the margin;
so coax the syllables to pronounce a line
thriftily with the pitch and twist
of spirits twittering in the dark wood.

Air the phrasing, diversify it, intrigue
unconditionally heart and mind;
the aura disappears whenever
there is no kindness to strangers,

no fragile pergola for the descent
of the tomcat that hoots,
of the owl that coolly mews.

To juxtapose contraries in virtual time,
sharpening profiles, even,
words will move by speaking for themselves.
Collision as collusion returns to dust
desire whose object was to be transformed.
Let only two snails of perception lock horns
and the song-line runs with zest.

Then as a person the poet disappears,
to be heard inside his language, as a voice:
it could be communing or conversing –
speech as of a soul that looked around and keenly,
if in vain,
for news so good as to be disquieting.

The poem startles words out of their holes,
let no hushed and Sunday voice shoot the breeze,
when the poem crackles, fire and ice,
it is a sort of chant, but parlando,
a parley, or a party, in a conflict zone,
where any right good sparrow,
scuffling for food, does forgetfully swoop
while flying out its line in a state of bliss.

What now if, in the South-West,
all this fine European baggage,
packed by Mother, still by her sins
is falsified, infected? We spoil like apples,
whole selves wizened by distraction and stress.
In their ruin, these stacked cavern dwellings,
solid hearths of civilisation once,
restored to the Great Spirit its rough gift,
a multitude of life, less grudgingly
than we may do when our turn comes.

1892   Aloysius Bertrand, petit-fils.

Two Squibs

1

Mariolatry No
Man of letters, Richard Chevenix Trench,
in Eighteen Forty-Nine,
published his choice of Sacred Latin Verse,
which was all very fine
except that, as an Anglican bishop hostile to Rome,
he made a good thing worse.

Judging the Virgin to have been a wench,
Trench, in his manly devotions touchy as mimosa,
excluded from his tome
the 'Stabat mater dolorosa'.

2

Looking Back
Seen, what a roadside
    bomb does
and an avalanche
    of avarice;
but into a puddle
    as whimsically
as a bird will
    dip its beak
to drink,
    Alice Liddell
might have blundered,
    and never did.

Coda

In the distance a great cluster of domed red rocks rose up, a sort of mesa but sloping back from a scarp with deep clefts in it. Between those rocks and the high slope where we stood, with no level ground underfoot, an immense plain extended in clear light, with horses in the middle distance on the shoulder of a road that bisected the plain. All of a sudden these horses, there were four, began (gladly) to gallop, urged by their riders, and from close to where we stood somebody shouted: No! Stop them!

Somewhat lower on our slope, no more than 200 paces from where we had gathered, there were buildings. Some were ruined, some indistinct with age, some fresh and occupied. We had been housed there earlier, as guests of the châtelain. It was perhaps his voice that had shouted. Or perhaps the châtelain was this robust old man who now mounted the slope with a companion. In no time they reached us.

The châtelain's companion was a sturdy person, too. As he walked closer, I saw the slender book he was holding, and it had a title on the front cover, printed in large white capitals: *The Opus of Philip Tarquin*. Now the companion, with his straight face, grizzled hair closecropped, was to be introduced as the gentleman appointed to direct our film.

Clustered around him, we waited for an invitation, and, since nobody stepped forward, I approached him. Aiming to meet with him eye-to-eye, I missed his outstretched hand at first, but in an instant held it and shook it, announcing my name, Bertrand, Aloysius Bertrand. The hand I held was large, warm, dry, and rough, the hand of an English gardener – which was reassuring.

Then I walked up the slope and squatted on the patchy grass, waiting for the next thing that might be about to happen in this fascinating and spacious place. For I was worried that the companion might crush all the magnificence, of the red rocks, of the luminous plain, of the horses, of the château, into a bed-sitting-room à la Tarquin. I was left admiring the distance, wondering if this was north Arizona or south Utah, the land again of the Navajo.

Manchild, always haunted by a sense of loss, I lost no primal dream but relinquish its lookalike, the mirage, recompense for the evils born of anguish. A gust of wind brings with the scent of pinyon woodsmoke one or two memories, and then the movement of memory itself. It is as well to be here. I act on impulse. I will slip away and on horseback, in another light rediscover cities I lived in, beaches I combed, people I mingled with, surely not so long ago.

Frescoes with Graffiti

The Transfigured Don Juan

Through kingdoms and republics
    a heartbeat carried me,
through the long conversations,
    lucid and turbulent. Floating
through books, I would also gavotte
    through vistas of topiary,
into a lavender attic,
    into the nook of the girl I was mad for.

I was carried across great waters,
    through the air and cities in ruins,
nonchalant, elevated, untouched by cafard;
    a very bottle of vintage sensations
I rolled abroad, a heartbeat drove me
    to distraction in zoological gardens,
prehistory I imagined, unbottled
    the beauty of animals, paint or flesh.
I was also a sort of a dog, at best;
    then for combat with dog and bottle
came indiscreet women.

How much more might be said,
    and to write is delightful,
for the sea, all by itself, comes to mind,
    the sea insensible of star and compass:
there is a restlessness at the back of creation,
    while it stormed, I made peace with it.

Now the heartbeat is calling for medicine,
    and a murk could curdle the blood.
One touch of its favourite liquor
    and heart recoils; a mere touch,
I'm sorry to say, gives me a bad moment;
    blood has begun to act as a jealous devil.

Then I am alone, dizzy with me,
        a rain of dots, blue as convolvulus,
bespittles everything in eyesight.
        Also to die is not delightful,
it is hardest not to fear, never again
        so to enjoy hilarity,
bodies in motion, expressions that linger
        on faces, the hum
of voices among the wines,
        a holy hush dividing the voices:
they say the kite of Transcendence
        has a long, long fluttering tail.

Imagine then bitterly, bitterly believing
        that you fumbled in turbulence,
misjudged in lucidity; for flightily
        in each you were halfway neither, at most
(and the slave to ego never foils an ignorant
        hate that lays its curse on the world);
besides, only now, as I climb these quaint stairs
        to the threshold of the college of ghosts,
do I put those words to them.

Near Oblivion

Near oblivion
a strange excitement

visible through a gap
in needles of juniper

past a sunlit
white stone wall

twice a person strides
quite detached.

Then rescued from a dream:
a speckled yellow bird
glided through the grass,
cupped in both hands it did not panic;

a pamphlet left behind
which had at all costs to be read;

a metal ashtray, bent,
etched along a bulge:
Paradise Lost.

Volta

Still you can see
the Holstein
cart horse

a frozen road,
driven
into the huge

chestnut buttock
an iron spike

and the brimstone
butterfly

at the sea-side
trembling

on the cap
of her lifted knee

A Construction for Gnostics

They spoke from the start
of a serpent uncoiling;
of the dark that took
activity from their cities,
they said it coiled up
and up like the serpent.

There was the good, there was
the evil. There was no break
for daylight between them,
and for the good of the world
they have to contend. Giddily,
the land surveyor harries
the clerks in the Castle;
they fob him off with illusion,
and with clowns for distraction.

A spiral is what became
of the old snake, a spiral
that goes in one way
and comes out the other.
But there's a twin to this spiral:
it goes in the other way
and comes out the one.
Between the spirals
daylight gathers its masses.

And the dark is split down the middle,
and the surveyor rigs
his trivial instrument,
rigs it at each outlet
of the contrary spirals.
All space in its magnitude around him,
the surveyor surveils the Castle,
down to the darkest closet.
At each tip of the spirals
something or other goes in,

and how it comes out
is cause for amazement.
When evil goes in, rottenness
takes a whirl among men,
and it will stain
the lapse of time, all of it,
till the good gets better.

In our confusion we argue
that evils deliver the goods;
if so, then the goods must
deliver the evils. If only
the lapse of time did not deform
the infoldings of such commerce;
if only daylight was limpid,
if only night was a lullaby.

It goes without saying
that the spirals, quite separate,
interact; there are evils
for us to inflict on each other;
yes, the genders thrive on a want;
a groundlessness, not evil
but (though wise men do not say)
a dump where doubles of it prosper.

Sehnsucht

Singularity – change position,
full moon regardless looks after
the Oak, the Temple, the Antelope.

Spasmic multitude –
a deluge of dirty ghosts
will mar the azure.

People group and fight.
Brawls disperse the just society.
While small talk traps the newborn,
among earnest poets ego runs amok.

Family smashed by heavy gunfire,
glowing smithereens of a mosaic,
beside his oven the baker's pelvis,
brushed and brushed, comes to light.

Defaced or broken, a few inscriptions;
bone splinters underpinned an agora;
at rock bottom, some original implements.

To have heart, to give soul, to keep quiet,
out from your hiding place, ever-young,
Lady, come remind us how.

An Ephemerid

The fight in it, it gives all it has got.
So what is to be done about this runt
of the daddylonglegs tribe who comes

nocturnally to skitter over the table top?
Quick as thought it prances about, squats
briefly on the white card, then picks up again

legs and wings that have no weight.
Light panics it into settlings and flights
nobody could predict, and here's a human

judging these to be actions without cause;
it is like the tales the idiotic memory
confides to consciousness. The runt,

can there exist a taxonomy to accommodate
such a dance of life? What remote control
drives it to behave even a bit like us?

Its element is not the heart of a storm;
no wonder the stream of light maddens it;
it is too mortal to be reached by a pang.

I swat it only now that it comes again,
as if it searched me out, but that is no less
an accident than every breath that batters it.

Calligraphy

Nut-brown, nothing on but a bikini,
the child runs gleaming from the pool;
a huge wind aired the quilt of linden trees,
aroused to sunlight, cat arches his back.

Poets, too, had to endure in ancient China
wars to beat or woo the barbarians;
as an ink of shadow spilled across the border,
they depicted in calligraphy the reverse.

Sacred King and Drunken Boat

1

Why did I send out my messengers
in all directions? On their kings
and on their deceptions it was not enough
to waste no words from a throne so sacred.

When the doors flew open, cornered
I did not make a speech, either.
It was their words winged like bullets
and their conceit that shot me down.

So God and I were in the same boat.
To me he entrusted the rudder;
and an odd thing happened, my hands
were ghostly now but I steered straight.

I steered and God navigated us
night and day downstream to the delta;
the rest of our journey was told
by a prodigious boy in an old poem.

Much of that time God was silent.
Now and again he pronounced questions.
There was no way to tell
whether or not he understood my answers.

Have they learned anything at all from history?
Was I at fault when creatures set themselves on fire?
Lost their minds, their families, their countries?
Could you not limit the ravages of the righteous?

It was a relief when the boy took over,
he brought along a whole flock of golden birds,
tempests of future, phosphors, archipelagoes,
fermenting surge, starburst of a herring shoal.

And what ivory parapets could he swarm over
as oceans appeared, there in his bleak room;
they rose out of his impossible longing
for a pond with a toy boat in it, back home.

2

Return for me there is none,
no return to the Pool of London,
to me with a mop of tawny hair,
my body alive with working muscle.

I will not come again, nor can the grey brick
ribbon-hovel stand there in line
on the way to the docks. Domesticity,
it reeked of fog and cod.

I'll tell instead of the night
when the boy was talking stiffly;
how I paid a penny, so he could drink;
his list of words, the voice reciting them.

All day in the dock driving rivets in,
but then he believed me when I confided
that in a dream once I heard a voice
say in a clear tone: Christ was a sailor.

Forlorn his face, even more so
when I had told him such a secret:
'From zy pool of Londres gone zee bo mariners.
Alors! Eet steenk laik a pool of sheet.'

Homage to Renoir

It is a long time since I saw a motleybird
flit from one perch to the next
on a stone wall or in a hedge alongside
when I happened to be passing

What years pass and pass what years
and that rare beast is a bird of passage
to be believed even when unseen
with its plumage ultramarine and emerald

with its golden crest on the alert. Species
appear like wrens like partridges
all the sizes arise from beyond our ken
to occupy mere points of a pig's bristle
where states of mind clashing still
or now harmonious are singled out
and immensity perspires the gloss
if not the waste of our surrounds

Impossible and probable
improbable and not at all absurd
the motleybird has no explanation
is there and it is not and there it goes
naively apt and fiercely strict
from any moment to the next

With a sol-fa canto it swoops as a hawk does
it comes and goes but level
if you plod up or down the road
trodden out by ancient cattle
soldiers and pilgrims in their time
all day till swallowed by the dark

In the daytime it nests
like any other bird but in a globe
of grasses with their distinct odours
grasses and twigs to buttress them

and the nest is lined with the down
of feathers they collect

The young are never to be seen
slow in growing they are sequestered
they fly out full-feathered next Spring
all gold and blue and ready to go
singing polyphony with every note
distinct as a bell

into the wild they go into domains
unique and peculiar to the winged
where a place is breath drawn
where noises cannot penetrate
where the motleybird finds time to roost
with rather a graceful rustle

                    From there
it brought the news to Chuang-Tzu
to Li Po and Kublai Khan
Auguste Renoir and Prospero

No Say

The collectivisers take the streets
tumbrils arrive, the waltz goes on.

Here is the gate of solid stone,
my friend walks up as I dismount.

His house is here, behind the gate,
there will be luncheon up that hill.

The gate's on fire, my friend is gone;
the tumbrils roll, the waltz goes on.

Take your time, catch your breath;
in these concerns you had no say.

Three thousand miles from his Emperor
intrepid Chang stumbled on some Greeks.

Something is squirming up the stair;
the window opens, I'd better wait.

A Bird Lantern

Before nightfall
the emptiness
in the glass cube
above the residue
of mixed seeds
in their dangling
oblong feeder
fills for a time
with amber light.

Souvenir of Hamburg, 1946

Quite ruined buildings
were there to surround it.

It bisected a ruined block
between the carpark and the canteen.

She who places her bare feet
one after the other on the shore,

she had required this narrow street;
lowly spectres of her, in turn,

required that it be out of bounds.
Sexual organs set a scene

for the exchange of cigarettes;
half a dozen spuds

paid for lips to suck you off.
The barefoot girl, whose powers

stormed the earth, made heaven false,
poetry better when oblique,

ah, for her what a fall from grace
that taboo pool of bodies was,

which for us boys in blue or brown,
fresh or foul, was just a hole.

Near Lakenheath

Their western eyes might blink at this spent devil
        but watch his cherries ripen:
disturbers of received opinion,
        discoverers
in things we care about,
        of the finer angle, richer resonance:
unflustered by trivia, serene
        votaries of paradox:
their roll of honour
        reaches back to Prometheus.
Gadgets now embalm
        the names and histories
(an avenging angel has not yet
        cleaned the slate).
No, from this fragile cup
        in the hands of commerce –

liquid all must crave,
       toxic with platitudes –
some bodies of intelligence
       do fly beyond the rim;
then as we plunge through loss,
       cruelty, and catastrophe,
how should your precious fictions,
       the fullness of time,
the fullness of being,
       still maintain a form
for more than a solitary?

★   ★   ★

Devils below your hearthstone
       do not think again;
but this one did so, twice.
       They are incorrigible.
They do not care for facts
       and when minds move
inconstantly to mask small, glorious
       and vicious desires,
it does not puzzle them. Big devils
       have no mind of their own:
driven by the blind force of nothing,
       their thing is to be self-possessed.

This devil rode all night astride the backbone
       of his turtle thought, and then
they stopped for oats at Lakenheath. The plain
       heather was still blue and white,
in sunshine for once the curlew overhead
       played his oboe mournfully.
Inside the ground, yes, inside it, here and now
       blunter the flaked flint
scrapers lay, in their elegance fashioned
       to fit the fingers poised over animal skins;
and here were the axe-heads and the hammers
       for fitting bivouacs. Not so deep

348

silver dishes shone, wrought with figures
        of gods dancing, in delicate relief,
skilled handiwork also, and the wine bowls,
        lachrymatories of blown glass.

★   ★   ★

Suchlike were relics of a villa built
        before the Empire crumbled.
We may suppose a family lived there for generations,
        then Saxons had their turn, swarming
across the land, tunics held fast
        with small bronze clasps,
voracious, merciless. Their havoc weighed heavier
        whenever British weather hit hard.
Once more from Sunrise barbarians had come,
        a power anon, another house-plan.

★   ★   ★

(De rerum vibris loquitur tunc latro ipse:)

The tide ebbed over the Skaggerrack
        and left in rock pools
the cowrie, the fish writ minuscule.

Be seated, watch the Cereus bloom
        spreading, open, a golden juice
glistens there. On time, once a year, now
        the big moth flies. See it settle.
Be silent for its drinking is profound.

To send an assailant packing
        the deep-sea spinning shrimp
evacuates a phosphorescent mass
        longer than its body.

A manifold of models also attests to change,
            exfoliating painlessly
nocturnal wonders never crowd upon us,
            never lost the arcane recedes,
magnet of our inventions,
            and over the arcane we throw
the garment of syllables, sparrows to haul
            Aphrodite's chariot also,
secret thistledown, meal for the goldfinch.
            No place inhibited the wonder,
it comes and goes, thus, it was thought,
            our mute Immortals
send their signs. Too soon we swarm,
            then gross conformity
catapults violence.

                    ★   ★   ★

Ground below the fans and croziers of bracken
            enveloped, just so, scraps of treasure.
These in this devil's digressions conspiring
            with memoirs of Maquisards
were models of resilience, quiddities deposited
            in the lost time, and in imagination,
real things of honest sweat and light of heart.
            An unappeasable spirit makes waves.

Almost ready to go, so it was told,
            a lesser spirit will project
the bracken sprouts, fans and croziers
            in their early moment, green,
then turning darker, gold. Peace
            is all, so images may pass
in every detail, radiance fuels
            an exchange of passions
among the bodies; all is enigmatic
            but at peace and festive,
a simplicity lightens the heart. This devil
            hears of no such bliss,

nothing holds fast, though it is frozen
        and the music makes no promises
but of conflicts between pleasures at being
        born mutable. Yet by such ground
beneath bracken green or gold,
        the bracken of fans and of croziers
not gone to waste, might just as soon,
        when Fortune savages the powers,
though war may be just,
        our dead be clad in barleycorn.

The Race Across the Quicksand

A little rose bush in its tub
had been pruned back
so thoroughly it looked
to visitors irreparably stunted.

        It is willing still;
ovals, every which way tilted,
emerald and deep violet leaves
stream from stems that push
up and up.

Smiling to herself,
    Something about it,
        said the woman from Bethesda.

One beanpole of a stem
for days and days has had
one tight shut bud on top;

                and the roots pump
now there's no way to stop
a gush of air that waits
to steal the scent of it.

From Our Imagery of Early Greeks

Bright-eyed, above average,
never vulgar, all-of-a-piece

Nude in a gym, boys grunt and grapple,
men dawdle, draped, in colonnades

Imagine how they might have danced
their maze of contradictions out

Early Greeks, quite at home
with gods they had to wrestle with

Dynasties brawled, the primal rapture
sparked a thought of civil freedom

From one of them the peacock rose,
music to worship by, and mania

Human waste, the stink of it,
achieved a gusto in their speech

The starlit ship creaked safely home,
still darker things they knew about

(In the course of time they'll ask
what is behind the past behind us?

Gods? Ourselves? Did their names
magnify powers we have at heart?

Through us they feel; if we falter,
what happens to the price of bread?)

Identity embraced their bodies,
the slow light carved cube or oval ·

They did not cram with wings and thrones
an afterworld that burgled heaven

Nose to nose, chopping flesh,
whatever it was, they fought it out

No future penalty to reckon with,
like ears of wheat our grains are knit

With measure. Dance-steps of the gods,
hear still their faulty cosmos hum

They lift, astonished, their human gaze
from figured bowls to first blush on the crests

Remembering Johannes Bobrowski (1917–65)

Carefully Lucy removes her toy bone
from the basket Caspar the Black annexed.
Here Miranda fingers on her guitar
difficult harmonies in Tarrega's Romanza.

Paco the freshly shorn long-haired other cat
curls up grey and white here on the couch,
curls his bushy tail round folded paws;
here, up and down, for breath his stomach goes.

Here too the vase and yellow jasmine in it
detain the sunlight, so does the snow outside.
Again with envy I watch how easily
Paco's abdomen goes up and down.

Just so the bones of Johannes Bobrowski
have shed his flesh, the skull shows over there
and his Vistula whispers on, separately trees
come into leaf across towns missing their Jews.

Perkun, I pray you, let me not imagine
on his groin a somnolent slug, grubs eating him.
Let his clavichord answer still the call of his fingers.
He was a deep one, let it be known, when writing came.

Old Shrines

Here comes the huge always toppling
crest of the wave of time,
and from across the courtyard erupts
a song to the drumbeat, presleyan,
and sung to a dull routine.

And here's the thought of shrines,
those old shrines we saw and haunted
our first afternoons in the Vaucluse,
one or two sarcophagi in the precinct,
old Saint Pantaleon.

Even more so, beneath a little altar
on a slope of the elephant mountain,
she had been curled into marble,
a long-haired mermaid, long ago,
Magdalene, who washed the feet.

Shrines, forty years later – and
here's one who calls to the Visigoths
but gave ear to the silly song
that penetrates the loitering
air of an undisturbed neighbourhood,

one who has given thanks for those
who rose from the almighty mud
and quarried stone for shrines,
who nosed out good locations, crawling
also free from the designs of luxury.

It was the shrines, in simple places;
you could pass by, notice nothing. Or
a time of day, a certain light
freed you from all shame. The shrine
with a warm dry hand guided memory,

guided it to a vanishing point, a
threshold in the brain-cells
of the shrine-makers. They must have
felt deep down into a place
for the electric thread and mysterious

spring that had to be, surely,
secreted under the crust of the planet.
Natural power marked the spot;
simply a feeling for its holiness
also grew with remembrance of martyrs.

Now there's a sense of something
infinitely secluded but to be discerned
circling a shinbone,
calling from a stopped phial
without so much as a bloodstain in it.

'If From The Distance...'

The Lydian tomb with its arched roof
puts a limestone boundary round itself.

Sardis grew boundaries for time and space;
this little horse of jet a Zuni Benvenuto

cut into shape does not break loose
from its place on the lid of a cigar-box.

It is as if things put boundaries round themselves;
it is as if we did it for us, who else.

The boundaries meeting, coming to an agreement,
Fortunate Isles of intelligibility lure our ships.

If there is no agreement, I suppose,
less and less comes to be intelligible.

Then it is as if, without boundaries,
things do not stay put, they take their distance,

so lost in distance that we pay long visits
to self-conceit, and usury, and slavishness.

So Hölderlin's poem, 'Wenn aus der Ferne,'
did it simply peter out? Or had,

while he was copying words a spirit uttered,
though a tomb for twenty years consumed her body,

mad Hölderlin's eyes filled with tears,
leaving nowhere to place the goose-quill's tip?

Go with Isaac Rosenberg

Afternoon moves on
air now so warm

Among the thin green
pipes of the bamboo

those twitters come
from the chick sparrows

It is tentative, a touch
of air all over skin

Bless, the word for it
becomes the thing

Go with Isaac Rosenberg
scavenging on the Somme

'Sometimes I find a bible
in a dead man's clothes

'I tear out pages that I want,
and carry them around with me.'

Among Signs

Two red eyes in the second light:
naked I stood in a great crowd waiting
to wash and get dressed.

No imminent threat, the police
would never be so colourful –
the eyes were flowers hanging from a vine.

Bright orange red trumpet flowers.
Soft miniature old phonograph horns.
Xerxes commanding, sound the charge,

let our battle begin. The rest –
business cycles, decreed and logical,
warring without end – was history.

Innate, this doubling of an object has you
thanking that you don't permanently bite
your lip, wondering what is this or that.

Or neither, there being no other negative.
Riddled with superstition you plant
flowers in a garden of make-belief. They

keep faith, never wicked. With one look
they affix their spell; the naked know
it is high time to wriggle out of bed.

Then a sea-shell, a voice calling, chimneys
clustered in a fog, lower nets, wait,
and haul the one, the hesitator, in.

On the Futility of Pathos

Concerning freedom
many poems,

noble poems
metaphors

of lovers, even,
of embracing,

of freely
galloping horses,

of horses
Anatolian

blue freedom.
Deep in pain

breathily voices
implore;

but freedom
is whole,

camps and prisons
bits and pieces.

Whole, it deserves
no imploring; even as

oppression sucks,
captivity breaks backs,

we listen, listen
for the right note;

a free speaker
will distrust statistics,

speak not of a work-force
but of the young somebodies,

of constructive conscience
undulled by functions.

His tranquillity
prompts right action.

He hardly cares for any
but the actual facts,

and he will explore,
explore freedom's violations

and how it is elusive, even
when it is fought for

by those who wait,
able to mind it justly.

(Clipped whispers
wide of the mark –

the lone horse pines for the herd,
chafe at your bond in each embrace.)

Haikus

1

Basho

Old pond quit of ice,
new frog poised to jump; hear then
the sound a plop makes.

Kikaku

Tiny green tree-frog,
his trip by banana leaf,
take it easy now.

Miss Chiyo of Kaga

There's the pail, but, hush,
in morning glory's embrace.
Ask for one next door.

2

Many mundane cares,
night and day the sparrows fuss:
Where's food? Where shelter?

★

The long-lived grapple
with the brevity of life;
only time will tell.

★

A feather floats down,
already the hawk forgot
picking clean the bones.

★

Eudaimonia:
wiser now, ocean beauty
swings out, finds the stars.

3
Alcman (fl. 630 B.C.)

Purple, sacred birds,
age withers me, in my place
skim those flowers of foam;

★

so the halcyons did
for Alcman what birds will do,
while there is yet time.

★

The Mockingbird

One sip and he tilts
high his beak; down his gullet
feel a moment go.

361

Poems Without a Subject

1

                    Backward old snake
                  persecutions none
               wounds none
            prison none
         exile none

does despair
   does shrug
         does grieve
            does rage
               does dither

                     and delight
                  that Montaigne
               annotated heavily
            his (Lambin 1563)
            De rerum natura.

2

In a dram h saw th qun of havn
a dmoisll sh was, a Frnch on

With hr holy fingr sh pointd comically at him

If this wr a ral pom it would b mystrious.

3

    otus
    frog on it
    anguishing

    soon
    pops
    into the poo

    so do sous
    into the word
    beow.

4

Private lie:
Take
shelter, ight o
even
ast
idious
in
truders.
Everywhere
ind
riends.

Two Antiques

in memory of Enrique Granados,
composer of the Caress Waltz

1

A Riddle: On Hearing the Shouts of Children
from their Playground

Attach no name to this tall shrub,
its branches were not made to swarm,
vertically up they shoot, gaps between
make space for leaves purple as plums –
each branch, each leaf, looks individual.
The topmost leaves (fancy them senior,
as if their sharp angle moored,
earliest of things, desire for the light)
flare up, aslant, all but perpendicular.
Only the lower leaves lie flat and cradle
spherical raindrops, at random,
glittering diamonds, two or three.
Night comes, fear death if you must,
all this you still can see.

2

Sixteen Ounces for Shylock

Uncertainty, let me still walk at ease;
I move, but am not moving as I please.

The cyclist treads andante up his hill,
days from now he will be treading still –

I foresee my absence from this airy bench,
no-one to wink at every passing wench.

What earth is not elsewhere, or perhaps
décor for memory drained and dunces' caps?

(Should diggers find this tablet, they will grin
at the spindly letters and the funk I'm in):

O intestinal chaos we endure,
raving in ecstasy, banal in pedicure,

I branched from you, not the real root at all,
now it's too late, I am beyond recall.

Justice, prevail; my last act I'll rehearse
with sufficient savvy to revoke this verse.

On Two Strips of Parchment

1

This solitary and suspended
oblong bird-feeder
this first warmth in January still
this clear blue early day
this single finch looking out
from her perch

simply enjoying life

This unrest
this prospect of distance
circumscribing the unrest
of a desire to apprehend
through the creature
the Signature

inked into a wingbeat

2

Silver-haired, chatting
in a corner of the courtyard
that sunny afternoon,
their heads,
their arms and legs
litter the asphalt.
Home late; a room reeks
of cobbler's wax
(can Hawking have exploded Boehme?)
so he must again
be careful where he puts his feet.

Items in a Showcase

(*Musée des lettres et manuscrits*)

Every single one of them fitted sideways
into the pocket of a waistcoat;

these are the cartes de visite
of an immense variety of persons:

forgotten notables, in their time
guillotined by the same hangman.

Portrait heads and shoulders – a host
of unquestioning expressions; even if

the faces were still innocent or frozen
for the photograph, each has its own

mystery or blush. Cheery old bourreau,
you were so proud of this collection of yours,

almost a hundred excellent breeds
any one of which you could have taken

out of your waistcoat pocket, itching
to tell the story over an eau de vie.

Or, secret philanthropist, you kept them all
for the sake of some you knew might not be guilty.

Rilke on the Street

Apex of the human pyramid,
the smile of the acrobat child.

Çanakkale

All but a century
gone. By the thousand,
pinned down
on slopes, on beachheads
shot to death, and rawboned,
ours and theirs, blown
to pieces.
        Two-faced anthropos,
late again, stirs to condemn
the bad plan, but snatches a caress:
        Now, unmarked,
that fish
once on this opposite shore
for who knows who to remember,
scales glistening in a shell
of late sunlight, a savage
to the last gasp,
the writhing amorous, beheaded,
gutted, eaten.

Three Translations

Prometheus Saxifrage

for Denise Nivelle

(Touching Hölderlin's Aeolian hand.)
(after René Char)

What would reality be without the disruptive energy of poetry?

Living among us God was too powerful. We no longer knew
how to be moving on. Stars sovereign in his eyes are
dead in ours.

These are the questions of angels, provoked when the
demons broke in among them. They fastened us to the rock,
to thrash us and to love us. Over and over again.

There is one single struggle and it happens in the dark.
Victory is on the fringes only.

Noble seed, battles, and the good will of my neighbour,
with my hunk of bread I'll protect you from the dawn
that is deaf, while I wait for the day of high rain,
of green lemon, which for those who burn, for those who
are headstrong, surely will come.

[*La parole en archipel*, 1961]

Zbigniew Herbert

Claudius the God

(translated in fond memory of Zbigniew Herbert
during his Berlin years)

I spoke Greek like an Athenian but respectably
kept a lookout for what was not Greek to me
nature started me off
but did not complete me
a wagon driver educated me I was thrashed
needled even in testaments I was made fun of
at a ripe age I enjoyed the reputation
                              of a gambler and drinker
I liked the suburban hobbledehoys and tarts
I played being an idiot for fear of death played
            patiently and for a long time
silliness slips easily into the bloodstream
after Caligula's murder I hid behind the curtain
the Praetorians dragged me out
when the world was flung at my feet
I didn't even have time to put on my face
                              a look of intelligence
since then I have drudged tirelessly I was a Hercules
                              of administration
every day I issued dozens of condemnations
                  announcements decrees
I was most of all proud of the rule that
                              at dinner parties
it was permissible to emit belly-noises
who'd have the cheek to call me a tyrant
unjustly I'm reproached for having been
                  cruel and cynical
actually my thoughts were elsewhere
after Messalina was murdered I asked at dinner
why is the lady of the house not present?
                  there was deathly silence
                        I'd clean forgotten

I had new aqueducts constructed
after that it was easy in Rome to wash
                 the bloodstains away
if the historians and keepers of death-lists
                        are to be believed
I condemned to death 35 senators
                 and 300 tribunes
I won't deny it it's possible
but I did it all to take from death
                 its air of inescapability
I had the dead invited to a dice game
and if they didn't come I punished them with fines

I enlarged the bounds of my empire to include
        Britain and Mauretania and also Thrace
                        or so it would seem
but my triumphal arch consists of letters
        with which I enriched the alphabet
I enlarged the bounds of speech the bounds
                 that is to say of freedom

Death was brought to me by Agrippina and
                        a passion for mushrooms
for me the mushroom the essence of the forest
                        became the essence of death
by the letters digamma and antisigma supported
                        under the arms like Oedipus
I tottered into the dark boondock of Orkus

[From the German version by Karl Dedecius, 1974]

Avowal

(after René Char)

Girl whom these old walls cannot possess, fountain
in which my solitary monarchy sees its image, how
would I ever be able to forget you since I have not
a thing to remember you by: you are the sum total
of time present. We shall be joined without having
to approach one another, without having to foresee
one another, as two poppies make a giant anemone.

I shall not pass into your heart to limit its
memory. I shall not constrain your mouth from
opening on the blue of the air and the thirst to
get up and go. For you I want to be liberty and
the wind of life that blows across the threshold of
Always before ever night is nowhere to be found.

[*Poèmes*, GLM, 1969]

A Keeper of the Reliquary

> Thus is man that great and true *amphibium,* whose nature is
> disposed to live, not only like other creatures in diverse
> elements, but in divided and distinguished worlds...
>
> Sir Thomas Browne, *Religio Medici*

A Keeper of the Reliquary

I

At the Thought of Rilke

Certainly they exist, the flittermice,
so do insects they gobble quickly up.
We see them serving a single purpose,
they are blessed, with existences complete.

What are we doing with this dependence
on thinking of existence, as if
thought procured the fullness of it?
I heave at an existence to complete it.
The matter is penetrated once in a while,
and we do go about the business a short way.

The brevity hits hard on old age:
To stillness a beautiful object extends
but does not complete us. Night surge
of the sea, from here, safe on the shore,
prolongs desire, when Fortune walks barefoot.

Then we are fooled by our own transcendent
feeling, a depth, an atmosphere.
In creation's midst this body holds its own,
and the feeling glides into memory easily,
like fumes in motion, the confecting of a cake.

A cemetery by the sea is not assayed.
The grand phrase that would hold in their place

the fractions of a sensed thing puzzles us.
We have kept our heads down. The knock of booms,
chime of a silver bell, minute by minute
they die but are repeated.

II

Malatesta's Phantom

I don't want to feel
as old men tend to do
the pang
not to have been
in good times
happy enough at the good.
Happiness at the good
was attributed
to the old people once;
now the old do not forget
evils that poisoned even
the goods of civil society;
and mark my words, this pang
is for what we have not done,
even failure to appreciate
moments to the full,
delightful enrichments
of sexual union,
the sight of the boat keel
furling back the ocean,
the taste, with mint,
of a new potato.

It is no secret:
The living are bound to feel,
and feel from the cradle,
something is missing.
A chord or cadence in music
as it moved on, gave me,

a mere boy, such dread, as if
soul were a cavity
catching the echo
only to kill it. Soon
a dream would come
of making that absence good
by extending the cave
to accommodate
creations of a density
putting the hollows to flight.

Should old people
go on about it? Who
ever heeded the warnings?
Who reads sympathetically
the signs, who'll refuse
to wallow in twilight?

Did I, Malatesta, take it
to heart, to heart
that marble was slow,
exceedingly slow to be
compounded by its ocean
depths, that its atoms
advanced
from the back of beyond
at last to be modeled
exquisitely by hand,
hand and chisel, finishing
polished figures in low relief?

Did I recognise
that others would toil
at what I could not create?
Only my zest and legend
like vapour settle down.
Death with its ugly coda,
O questioners of mine,
was a delay once more

in the perfection
of my memorial to her:
before she was not there
I could not know the seasons
of a perpetual love.

So to resist
was Malatesta's choice.
With all the extravagance
of a nature like a bullet
that ricochets away, he chose
to get along as best he could.
Let the chisel not falter,
let the marble come true.
How evil starts and spreads
let the craftsman make known.

III

Dissecting Shadow

> 'of the first Chinese dynasties –
> amulets shaped as cicadas … '
>   Matila Ghyka, *The World Mine Oyster*, 1961

Costume cut from my own juice,
crisp as I enjoyed it,
soon the capsule split.

Birth, now I'm over-exerted,
this effort, the fracas,
those elements, they crush me.

But I stretch out, a leg, an eye,
all form, arisen, no time to lose,
from a shaft sunk in the earth.

Me, golden aura, I blaze the call,
up high, suspended somewhere,
into the absolute blue,

for soon I replicate, first
I warble for it, green, green,
ten thousand years ago.

IV

Token

They squeezed me into a tube
    with a hole at either end.
A lintel was underneath me,
    then they hammered me in,
not cruelly, no, breezily.

I blessed the house, I alone
    knew what I said;
slide me from the tube,
    unfold the roll of me,
my letters spell no noise.

As they will always do,
    they cut my throat;
if I could only bleat;
    now mute, I accuse
and magnify the Lord.

My first name I forgot;
    dust from a parched ravine,
I am spun, I adhere
    to the pad of a rabbit paw,
to a terebinth leaf.

The same dust purples dawn,
    then a sundown of cherry

and primrose deepens the murmur
    of women filling the streets:
my silence lost, again I begin.

V

The Lammergeyer

And did he best exist
forgetting that he existed,
for while the gravity of it spooked him,
there it was, the scarlet anemone –
what can it be reminding him of
but, remote as anything,
the ravine of Arnon in the depths of Moab.

We lost the path;
stepping among basalt boulders in the dark
we took in our hands the horses' tails.
The hoof knows nothing of figments;
they would find the way up and out.

The hard ground said it: errant selves exist,
and some, who knows, must move on unappeased.
Best hidden, driven by self-doubt,
he feared the scarlet anemone, it sucked him in,
his nightmare. And here it flowered,
in fellowship it flowered
from a crevice in the Roman bridge.
You look around – an expedition,
a peaceful expedition has plans of its own.

In such a ravaged narrative must figure
a great bird gliding, huge wings motionless,
close to the ridge where the horsemen halted;
it was afloat on a breeze, at eye-level,
plumage deep copper in the morning sunlight,
long copper tail perfect for a rudder.

VI

A Keeper of the Reliquary

Feeling there is no forward to go to
he stares at the huge Buick placard mounted
on the roof of the bar he quit moments ago
The noise of the traffic racket of voices
resemble not at all the reasonable murmur
such as warmed the smoky old Italian cafés
On a stone bench he recovers his sang froid
up there south-east a full moon à la Laforgue
flourishes its dime and chuckles piano
reminiscing of Artemis now her silver hounds
will be blazing a trail across the Sierras
Then she is the woman with fire in a hollow log
she moves at dawn from a distant sunrise and then
she has crossed the pusta and gone with the Danube
at last to arrive in the foothills of the Pyrenees
Back at him now she stares again as a black Buick
of which the magnified photo mounted up there
calls to his mind time's wingèd chariot
and it is J. Alfred Prufrock after all these quaint
nervous disturbances   First heard
one hundred years ago today the unsteady voice
dispelled a miasma of hushed bombast and pulverised
the gum then sugaring lyric speech in England
Abrupt changes of scene might have been naked truth
for hesitant people nonplussed by
the rush of inventions and threats to any singular
self   The touchy were drawn to the sea maiden
who pointed to a mossy torchlit cave – but how
first to expel a foul womb whence
the Persuaded crawl cocksure into uniform? –
honeycomb cell for venison and babies and
here come the hunters to die at thirty-five
but painting earliest images of posture
and movement in and among the animals
they copied and ate as gods, knowing all along

in their bones that play is the firstborn of time
Ah, Prufrock, soon to haunt the dim seminars
(the mutilated and the dead were absent)   This
moonlight, he could linger in it waiting to drown
when to the human voices he must wake again
Still the maimed and captives call nonstop
galleries emptied fill with fat bamboo
goblins riot round the hob but on the porch
there is a free man who talks with the fireflies.

Two Poems Mistakenly Omitted from
Collected Poems

The Child at the Piano

The child at the piano
plinking, planking, plonks.
I stare and stare. Twigs
angle the air with green outside.

Handfuls of notes, all happening at once,
her tunes do not occur; on their backs
round they whizz like stunned wasps; contour
would crush that kind of mass.

Telescoping flukes and faults, their
tenuous terrain dislocates
no spheres I know of. Her index rebounding
off high C beckons no hell boulder up.

The heroics, fatuous, ordain yet
this act's assumption of her whole element.
Boughs of sound swoop through the room,
happily, for her to swing from.

So I call my thought's bluff. My thumb
struts down the keys, too, pings
to her plonks, on both white and black notes,
while the green air outside lets us be.

(from *Nonsequences*, 1965)

January 1919

What if I know, Liebknecht, who shot you dead.
Tiergarten trees unroll
staggering shadow, in spite of it all.
I am among the leaves; the inevitable
voices
have nothing left to say, the holed head
bleeding across a heap of progressive magazines;
torn from your face,
trees that turned around,
we do not sanctify the land with our wandering.
Look upon our children, they are mutilated.

(from *Nonsequences*, 1965)

Three Tributes

The Lost Elegy

for Lars Gustafsson

Into that light of the first September days in Skåne
They walked, figures, singular in your elegy.

Into that light, a fusion of pearl and amber,
Folded around the dark rust of barn walls

The figures in your elegy walked, on the margin of
A woodland: living and dead, they walked in time,

Neither knowing the other dead or alive,
All afloat in the light of amber and pearl.

Nothing in the world more natural
Than to read of them in your book,

To know those living who went to the edge,
To know whose dead will come to meet them,

House in its field, woodland set apart,
Trees consuming the house, field a lifetime to cross –

And meeting you in the corridor I stopped
And said this was an elegy to be translated,

For the density of its matter was a delight
Which drew from living air figures to be transformed

And got them doing a dance on the threshold
Where grace and agony, house and woodland meet.

You nodded, not in the least nonplussed;
I had sketched your poem, you recognised it:

Now, finding the time, I have been combing the book
High and low, twice ten times over:

There is, believe me, no such elegy in the book,
Yet it ran to one and a half pages exactly.

As I recall the coupled lines, see the light,
Solid figures in their clothes, the house, the field,

And hear the line I did not know existed –
'Dance in the ring without fear of afterthought,'

Now can you smell the smoke from chimneys in Skåne,
Hear in a moment the voice die out?

(written c. 1992)

Gingo Biloba

(from Goethe's *West-Östlicher Divan*)

A leaf from this Oriental tree
Fresh-planted in my garden here,
Though it is shaped with secrecy,
Its meaning for the wise is clear.

Is it one vivid single thing
By self-division complicated?
So close does here a couple cling
That we behold just one created?

On these questions I reflect
To find an equable response:
In my songs don't you detect
That I am one but twice at once?

Excavated Poem

One parting glance
to your window, you
had returned it, soon
passing Fire Lake
and Hospital Street
we heard from the prison
matins going on.

With feelings mixed,
as once you had them too,
we were touched
and with the shivers heard
the thieves and murderers,
voices gruff,
chant the morning hymn.

(Eduard Mörike, from a letter of 25 September 1853)

Interim

The Path Long Overgrown

What is this reckless
little thing
a magnet for

swept back wings
a tiny Concord

and a cat's
crooked whisker
sprouts

out of each nostril
of the pointed nose

Where the wings widen
a lightning bolt
bridges them

not a sound
one scorching zig

zag
long a portent
in these Navajo lands

and of what ganglion
turning and turning

a paroxysm
the gaze unstilled
this fascination

vaporous cage fixed
for the stiffening
animal and petty

intelligence starved
by the abstract –

Look now, she will sing,
how the mobs get going
daily quicker footstep

of old, cottages to thatch,
a soul within and secret

divine things
always
further on.

Dilemma after a Serious Accident

'All mere complexities…'

The cocks of Hades, even mute,
Still they inform against me.

My birds will make me better
The wren will call to hear from me
Sing for my supper, mockingbird

Just now I have to call the landlady
And tell her how I decide.

I could hail the locomotive horn
Otherwise, after midnight.

Our Rain Crow

'Car no chanta auzels ni piula…'
Arnaut Daniel

How apt of this rain crow
as rain came pattering down
for our flowers on the fresh grave
to hoot from his haunted orchard
sotto voce twice.

Then a wave had crested, giving rise
to fields of force; foaming vortices
carpenter the island of Phaeacia;
liquid eye-beams, Greek and chisel
carve to measure the finest of ships.

'Some few accustomed forms,
the absolute unimportant':
thus E.P. on a distinct slant
(still at an early age)
plotting some real connections.

So it is, here for the oldest folks
who still can hobble by,
there is a dangerous dog proclaiming
his Ah Ah Ah. One rough day's ride
and the sea crashes ashore.

I see my orchard gone for good.
Antiquated, for a moment
reasonably trees revive. One single twig
or two blossoming would cradle
a twitter of linnets. Soon
the punctual cuckoo too must croak. If
a cherry reddens,

it is for air, also the choir
far out in France at first light
let fly with one voice overtopping all;
yes, in the accustomed form,
it was the oriole, his folded fluting
for dear life I now recall.

What sense do I make, shedding this skin?
Memory, had you none tougher hidden?
Ancient shipyard fantasm,
fantasm orchard, sacred ground;
the texture puzzles, there is disbelief.
I do perceive it, past denying
pedestals to my words, to our crow its rain.

Note: Rain Crow is the by-name, current in rustic Central Texas,
for the yellow-billed cuckoo.

The Wicker Chair

The wicker chair found cause to think
that a wicker cloud floated overhead

and if he had never quit the chaos
chaos could not exist

But the wicker was thinking of a river
and of the trees that grow beside it

visible fishes and twice a boatman
not finding his way back to Peach Village

for the wicker was mindful of willows, each
lifting a dome of foliage across the water,

shadow of a quality quite foreign
to furnished rooms a long day's walk downstream.

★   ★

★

Look back no more than long enough,
the landscape changes. Why burn tonight

the wicker bull rigged so painstakingly?
Ribcage rounded well, a thousand wands

went into it. Skull and haunches
bulge where the bones fit. These people

must know, in more ways than one, how
to thwart any harm planted in human skin.

The bull means to be fire, what a warmth,
the good smell will be remembered. We'll see

the power of air, donors of all seed
and foods receive the sign;

and here's the ash for us, we smear it
all over our poor flesh, to copy moonlight.

★   ★

★

A basket for the cat would not be as bad,
anyway to be braided, woven, extenuated...

So wicker told itself: I do recall a fire,
its ancient blaze tempered my free nobility;

I sought simplicity in a shellfish receptacle,
anything but a lifetime trodden or sat upon.

Tra-la, feel a tension. Even untouched,
harpstrings and engines of furniture hum.

Caducity

The Kirghiz Steppes
    in old photos
        crumpled brown paper

Garden of Hotel Asia Minor
    sparse lawn, at the centre
        the dry fountain

Steppes once with an earth spell
    (regardless of wars)
        could bind the traveller

Garden where in memory
    the tenant's lame wife
        serves breakfast with heart

All over crumpled brown paper
    the traveller was laying
        roll on roll of film

On sparse lawn a few friends
    and strangers we took pleasure
        in every next thing

Age stuns heaping regrets
    sparky crock still a puzzle
        missing pieces

It never hurts to love again
    of all pieces when
        did spirit steal that one?

Fragment for a Lost Girl

Even if I'd known what you wanted to hear from me,
I'd have disappointed you.
                              Only in the night,
toward a certain pitch
of loneliness,
                    believe me, the dark sweltered
a marvel for you.
                    A mockingbird was
inventing a song, it sang on and on;
not a note in imitation,
the song conjugated trills delicate and furious,
melodies broken beyond repair;
it sang to bring the thunder on
                              and it sang the more
the louder the storm, thicker fell
sheets and sheets of rain.

The Typesetter's Visit to Cavafy

Admit me to your apartment, Sir,
dim as it is.
Tell me whatever you wish
or would invent (though probably not
for the boys with rosy lips) not only
for us future ghosts of those who flew
winged for their moment with a great soul.

I've knocked, when might you let me in? Now
captivity among the aged ages me,
painfully the past is now and real. You knew
how it revolved and for reasons of its own
played dead, omitting us, who dwindle,
easy to charm – and the beautiful are pitiless.

Your very phrasing, Sir, plucks from mud
epiphanies; not only gods
engender things that shine. Well considered,
your word for Fool and Stranger
reversed the plunge, flighted the dolphin.

I knock only once more. What should I do,
if you are out? I'll not wait until from some
smoky bar or nastier haunt you
hurry back home.
Up to your ironies I am not. How mild
you might be, there, eyes horn-rimmed eyes
swivelling every which way;
but when your moment spoke, you were
the lamp itself.

How you did wangle your way
over chasms, step by step
where no trails led but those
you rediscovered, Sir, to kindle
anew shocks of recognition that had knit
their texts for ancient tragedies.
Resignation, now wink at it,
your charity lets go with a sigh,
and for Zenobia you had a heart.

Eurydice Perceived

> '...the singing insect whose records
> are inscribed in our coal-seams.'
> J.-H. Fabre

What if I never again for once could see
her strict small face brighten to a gift
What if I tipped the attic windows open
and never woke again to birdsong rushing up

Torched by curiosity even as I caught my breath
I let the forelock of a moment slip
so rare a time that idled is

A moment captured strikes you unawares
but grows a form gradually in afterthought

Wait: in immediacy akin to music
unlike music the moments change their form
And even music loved but heard distractedly
a ton of times weighs never quite the same

So in a shroud the figure lifted
                              now most herself
shocked by the light out there incipient
her gaunt features were shaping to smile

What end then spells out the stuffs in variance?
What were the words that came to grandfather?
  It is the quality of the affection
that carves in a mind the trace...

I trace values on a map until the end
Let the quality, gods, of my affection
go deep as the clarity of grandfather's eyes
When memory in a moment shifts its parallel
I'll see and hear again re-opening the question

Even if Eros with a tusk scatters her garden
O predecessors you who teach restraint
with the grasshopper's voice our whispers blend
yours console in the shadow of her pergolas

Notes

Poems 2006–2009

The Enjoyment of Shouting

'The Strategy of Apamea'
Source: Edwyn Robert Bevan, *The House of Seleucus*, Vol. 1, 1902.
Posidonius (Bevan's source) was himself an Apamean and Apamea was
a military centre in Syria under the Macedonian kings. Posidonius may
have intended as caricature what now appears as parable.

'Among Egyptian Cenobites'
Source: Louis Duchesne, *Early History of the Christian Church*, Vol. 2,
1912.

'Mole-Catching'
After celebrating Homer's Muse in his 'To the Reader' prefacing his
Iliads translation, George Chapman challenged his contemporaries:

> Forth then, ye moles, sons of earth, abhor her,
> Keep still on in the dirty vulgar way,
> Till dirt receive your souls, to which ye vow,
> And with your poisoned spirits bewitch our thrifts.

'Samuel Palmer's Ghost Goes Scavenging'
As an aspiring young painter Palmer befriended old William Blake in
the 1820s. The ghost quotes verbatim, with mid-17th-century
spelling, from a meditation by Thomas Traherne that remained
unpublished till 1992. I had in mind Samuel Palmer's drawings in his
'Sketchbook' (Trianon, 1962).

'The Pepper Brandy'
Golushkin figures in Turgenev's *Virgin Soil* (1877) as a parochial Peck-
sniff.

'The Enjoyment of Shouting'
Line 5 is modelled on a phrase in Ezra Pound's notes for the last cantos
(see Humphrey Carpenter, *A Serious Character: The Life of Ezra Pound*,
New York, Delta, 1988, pp. 864 and 866). Line 6 is a quotation from
Canto IV. 'Scamander' from *Iliad*, Book 21.

'Vestigios de España, 1936'
Some details are derived from George Orwell's *Homage to Catalonia*
(Secker and Warburg, 1938, 1951 ed., p. 113).

'The Laundress'
The poem describes a painting that is actually not a Goya but resembles
his later work so sharply that it can be mistaken for one.

'From Georg Trakl'
'In ein altes Stammbuch' is dated September–October 1912 and
appeared in *Gedichte*, 1913. The other poems, of May 1914, are among
many drafted but unfinished (*Dichtungen und Briefe*, Salzburg, Otto
Müller, Vol. 1, 1969). The translations are not paraphrases, but here
and there the originals were trimmed.

'Another Melancholy'
The poem is a reading of Max Ernst's large painting *Der Hausengel*,
exhibited at the 'Melancholia' show at the Neue National-Galerie,
Berlin, in 2006.

Slight Poems

'Roughly thus ...'
From Mallarmé's conversation as reported in Gordon Millan's *Les
mardis de Stéphane Mallarmé* (St.Genouph, Librairie Nizet, 2008).

'The Halving of France'
The syntax of the first group of lines follows that of Hölderlin's 'Hälfte
des Lebens' but capsizes his setting ('Mit gelben Birnen hänget ... das
Land in den See'). Cf. also 'The View Back ...'

Friedrich Hölderlin, 'When out of Heaven'
We have no exact date for this poem in Alcaics from the years of
Hölderlin's madness (i.e., after 1806). It seemed justifiable to translate
the title otherwise than the opening phrase. The German title is edito-
rial; it is translated literally, so as to profile the spiritual sense these
words would have had for Hölderlin. 'Heavensent' secretes a spiritual
sense, but, being profane and idiomatic, it also retains the original's
hints of good fortune, blue skies.

'The Saint Preaches to the Birds'
The image alluded to is a fresco in the Basilica of San Croce, Florence.

'Seniority (2)'
Five words are taken from Samuel Beckett's short prose text 'Ceiling' (photo of typescript in Anne Atik, *How it Was*, Faber, 2001, Shoemaker and Hoard, 2005) – 'with dread of being again'.

Just Look at the Dancers

An exclamation from 'N.' in Lawrence Durrell's book *Prospero's Cell* (1945) provided the title. She meant villagers dancing at Kastellani on Corcyra, April 1938.

'Over the Low Thresholds Turning'
Line 10 is taken from Maurice Collis, *The First Holy One* (Faber, 1948, p. 188). A poem by Primo Levi suggested the 'bridge' at the end.

I have thought it best to comment on 'Monostichs 1-17'. Actually, there are nineteen, but two are designated (for mischief) as 'spurious', meaning of doubtful provenance.

Strictly speaking, a monostich is an entire self-sufficient poem in one single line of verse. Accordingly, such lines are rare. The self-sufficiency would require a high degree of 'pregnancy' in the wording. For instance, in Apollinaire's monostich 'Chantre' the word *cordeau* means *string*, *water horn*, and *body of water*. (French being full of homophones. A marine trumpet is in view, a musical instrument with only one string.) Readers of Arthur Waley's translations may also have noticed that old Chinese couplets come to sound, sometimes, like successive monostichs.

That was not what I had in mind, after being asked for monostichs that would be transcribed into embroideries. Strict monostichs seldom occur in the series here, but some angular and irregular relations between phrases within lines and from line to line arose as I wrote loose monostichs successively.

The stop, or caesura, that was the thing. It ruled out the suavity that run-on lines can enjoy. Without breaking continuity, lines could jump their rails and procure strange semantic collisions. Correspondingly, pictorial space (allusion to Manet and Degas) blending into terrestrial space became at once a motif to dwell on.

Regarding 'Miss Cassatt's corbelic smoke ball' in the first spurious monostich, friends try to persuade me that in my source 'carbolic' had been misprinted. I still prefer 'corbelic', and Miss [Mlle] Cassatt would be the painter, Mary Cassatt.

Index of Titles

Index of First Lines